JUROR
#11

JUROR #11

A Memoir Of The Broken Justice System And Rising From The Trials Of Life

KATRINA ROBERTSON

Juror #11 © Copyright 2022 Katrina Robertson

For more information, email Katrinarobertson216@gmail.com

ISBN: 979-8-88759-262-6 (Paperback)
ISBN: 979-8-88759-446-0 (Hardcover)
ISBN: 979-8-88759-263-3 (Ebook)

Library of Congress Control Number: 2023900125

Dedication and acknowledgments

THIS IS DEDICATED TO MY numerous friends who have been through their own fiery trials and risen from the ashes. Thank you for helping me stand back up.

Thank you to my husband, Shane, for encouraging me to tell my story, making me feel like it was worth sharing, and leading the way by publishing your own books.

Thank you to my children; you have given my life purpose and taught me about God's unconditional love for me.

A word of acknowledgment to my three brothers. I love being your "big" sister. I'm so proud of all of you! To my two sisters-in-law, thanks for making my brothers even better!

To "Juror #2," thank you for taking time out of your day to take pictures in the courthouse for the cover of this book.

Thank you to the numerous people who helped me with the editing of this book, especially Katelyn Willetts with Refine to Shine Story Services, who I believe read over my manuscript enough times to memorize it!

To my "work family" who are more than mere co-workers. You guys deal with my crazy life daily and haven't even kicked me to the curb yet! I seriously could not ask for a more supportive group of people to work with. It's because of you guys that I've been able to both have a career AND step into the lives of others to offer them help.

And lastly, thank you to my Lord and Savior, Jesus Christ, who didn't promise He would never give me more than I can handle but instead promised to be with me as I walk through the hard things in life.

Preface

I BELIEVE OUR LIVES ARE made up of stories. Some stories fade into our memories. Some stories define us and change us. We all have stories that are worth being told, stories that will leave marks on the souls of others and be left to the generations behind us. Stories that will help us learn and grow. Martin Luther is quoted as saying, "If you want to change the world, pick up your pen and write." So, that is what I've done here. I've written just some of my story in an attempt to give an authentic voice to difficult life experiences. I've recounted the events and conversations to the best of my memory. I've used no names in this book except my own, only titles, as this is my story told from my perspective.

This book centers around my experience as a juror, but it is also my opportunity to share many of the other struggles I've been through. Although the time frame covered here is only five months, from the day I am notified of being called as a juror to when a plea deal is offered due to a mistrial, I reach back to other hard circumstances I've faced. Most of my battles have involved raising adopted kids from traumatic backgrounds. My biological children have presented me with many challenges as well.

Nearly everything I do in my life centers around my desire to fulfill a purpose, make a difference, and leave people and things better than they were when I found them. This was my goal even as a juror, but I walked away from the experience feeling like an utter failure. A mistrial lay squarely on my shoulders alone. The lives of my adopted children have also not played out as I had hoped, and it leaves me feeling as if everything was done in futility. I know this isn't true though, as I stand on the truths of God's Word and hang on to the promise in Romans 8:28 (NIV): "And we know that in all things God works for the good of those who love him, who have been called according to his purpose." Maybe God will use my story to bring about awareness of some of the flaws in our judicial system.

In the end, this book was a work of therapy on my part, but I do hope it can serve as a source of inspiration and courage to others facing seemingly insurmountable times. We all have them, and we can all RISE out of them.

A rare holiday with the entire family,
"bonus" daughter included.

Me with all my "babies."

Saturday, April 9th, 2022

IT'S A BEAUTIFUL SPRING DAY, and I'm busily rushing around with the final preparations for my daughter's wedding, which is to be held at our home. It will be a small, intimate ceremony, but that doesn't cause the stress of it to be any less. Although my life has been one big stress case for the past eight years, my stress levels have escalated recently.

Both prom and the rehearsal dinner for the wedding were last night. My son's out-of-state girlfriend has come into town for the prom. We're also hosting a Japanese exchange student who went to the prom with a family friend, a "bonus daughter" of mine. With the wedding, I had no time to be involved with the prom preparations. Normally, I would have taken the girls to get their hair and make-up done, helped with finding accessories, taken lots of pictures, and chaperoned the after-prom party. I had wanted our exchange student to have a memorable time, and I had also wanted to be there for my son, who had been very anxious about the event. I just couldn't this time, though; it is still tearing at me. My son hadn't even made it thirty minutes at the prom before he ditched it and went to his grandmother's house with his date. He'd been in tears. He just couldn't handle the overstimulating social scene. He hated himself for it and was embarrassed, and I hated it for him. *Couldn't life be easy for just one of my kids?*

Today, I also must get another son to a defensive driving class which was a requirement of the court after a wreck. This was his third wreck in about six weeks, and there would be no driving for him for a while. Still, I have to find a way to get him to and from the class, while getting the final wedding preparations done. Oh, and make sure he's back and ready for his role in the wedding.

Then there's the big stressor. Months before, my husband and I had finally admitted that we weren't equipped to meet the needs of another son of ours. He's severely intellectually disabled and has complex behaviors that are difficult to manage. We had built him a house next to ours and staffed him with caregivers, hoping that could be a long-term solution. His behaviors had continued to escalate, and he had become more aggressive and violent. It had been impossible to keep him staffed, and the stress had begun to affect me. I was losing weight, losing hair, and was just a general basket case most of the time. There was no place in the state willing to take him. All this had climaxed with him being stuck in a local hospital's ER for forty-five days straight. Yes, forty-five days. They had kept him sedated through most of that, just to control him, but they then stepped into my nightmare. There was nowhere for him to go.

In desperation, I made a Facebook post regarding his pathetic condition and asked that people and organizations be tagged and that the post be shared. I hoped to get the attention of people who might have the power to do something about the situation and raise awareness of the lack of resources for individuals like my son. The response I received was overwhelming. I was getting endless messages from other moms with no options, as well as messages from state senators and representatives, and of course, I also got laughable advice from well-meaning people.

But then I got a call from someone I was interested in speaking with. My mind wanders back to the conversation with him, and it still gets my heart pumping. He was from the Disability Rights Association (DRA) and wanted to know how they could help. I could tell he was leaning toward wanting to go after the hospital for the condition my son was in. "Wait just one minute. You realize we're in this predicament partly because of your organization?" I asked, unable to conceal my frustration that he would think this problem was at all the hospital's fault.

He stammered, "I'm sorry, ma'am. I don't think I understand. We're here to help individuals with disabilities not to be treated the way your son is being treated."

I was driving in my car and had to find a place to pull over. This conversation was about to get heated. "The hospital is not equipped to handle him. They have no options. He is stuck there because there's nowhere in the state equipped to take him. Why is there nowhere for him? Because organizations like the DRA keep shutting down facilities and removing funding for beds for individuals like him!"

"I'm sorry, ma'am, but I'm going to have to disagree with you. We try to get more funding for community support so these individuals can live with dignity within their communities. I can help you get the support you need for your son."

I was raising my voice now. "We had support! He had a caregiver 24/7. And do you know what kind of nightmare it was to find suitable staff for him? Every single day I had to worry if they were going to show up, leave early, or take him to involve him in their own family crisis. We even had one aide steal a car from us. This is a minimum wage paying job that's near impossible to get reliable, dependable people to show up for—"

I tried to say more but he cut in, "You could have requested two aides for him and aides that were better paid and trained. I can help with that."

"*No*! Stop! This is all ridiculous. Two aides are not the answer. A place where they can monitor him in a safe environment with access to 24/7 nursing care, trained staff, and the ability to use mechanical and chemical restraints is where he needs to be. Period. You guys go and tout these butterflies and rainbows propaganda to lobbyists about getting these people out of facilities and into the community like you're heroes of some sort. That's a feel-good thing to fight for but it's not reality. I nearly killed myself trying to keep my son 'in the community.' This is *not* what I wanted, but I got to a place where I had to admit that it was the best thing for him and others." I was now about ready to break down. I already dealt with self-loathing that I'd not been able to give my son the life I felt he deserved, but here was someone else basically telling me I should have done more.

"I'll just have to disagree with you, ma'am."

I was furious. "So, you're admitting that you do want to close down more facilities?!"

"No. No, I'm not saying that. There should be both options. I think there should be more effort to make the community option work."

"The slogan on one of your most recent publications says, 'Shut the door of every institution.'"

"No, I don't believe you're right about that."

I wrote myself a note to email him a copy of it with that phrase highlighted when I got home.

"The DRA gives the impression that the State is out there just taking these people from their families and putting them in institutions. That's not true. These people are there because their families, even with support, simply cannot care for them safely. I also want to point out that I don't like the word 'institutions' being used. I think you do that on purpose because it's a derogatory term from back in the '60s and '70s when those places were bad. Rather than shutting them down, they should have been fixed. Those places are home, a good home, for a lot of people. Without them, they would be on the streets, in jail, or dead. People can live with dignity in those facilities." I was shaking with anger at this point and my car was getting hot. I started the engine back up and turned the AC up while rolling down the windows.

"We aren't going to see eye-to-eye on this issue. I want to make myself available if there's any way I can help. You have my contact information."

"Oh, I'm sure you'll hear from me again. I doubt there's any help you can give me. Before we go, let me ask you one question. Have you ever personally cared for an individual with complex behaviors? Someone with both intellectual disabilities and emotional health issues?"

He didn't answer my question and told me to have a good day.

That conversation has stayed with me. The day after the conversation, the forty-five-day mark at the hospital, the hospital threw up their hands and called the police because my son assaulted a doctor and nurse. The officer who responded had seen my Facebook post and sent me a message to call him. I called him and he told me the situation. He now had the impossible task of figuring out what to do with my son. Coming home simply wasn't an option. In the end, the officer turned a blind eye to my son's disability, had the hospital staff file assault charges, and took him to the county jail. He called me apologizing profusely. He knew jail wasn't where he needed to be. He didn't know what else to do. I told him an apology wasn't needed. What other choice did he have? At least my son and others would be safe while he was in jail. Supposedly the State was close to having a place for him.

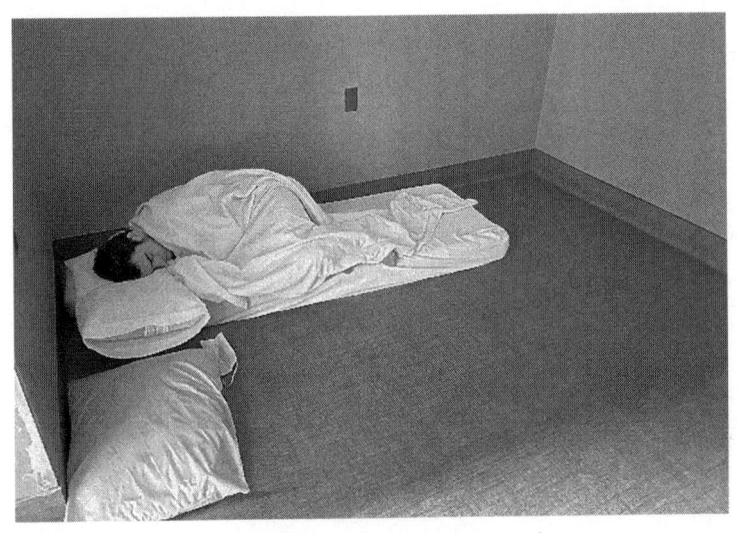

The picture that got the attention of many.

On this day, the day of the wedding, our son is now at a special facility in our state. I am receiving daily, sometimes multiple times a day, reports of "incidents" with him. *What if this place doesn't even work?* I have to push that thought away. The guilt I feel around the whole situation is almost more than I can handle some days. We had adopted him, and I feel like we've failed him. I have nearly killed myself trying to "save" him, and that guy from the DRA tried to make me feel like there was more I could have done.

We have another adopted son who also won't be at the wedding today. He's living somewhere in Florida now, and I haven't heard from him in a few months. If I allow my thoughts to linger on him for too long, the pain I felt when he first chose to walk away from us will resurface. The last time I'd seen him, I'd held him tightly and cried when he had opted out of joining us on a family vacation.

It's the wedding day, a day to have joy, right? Put your happy face on, Katrina, and keep your act together! There are so many details to give my attention to for the wedding. I'm making sure all our rentals are in place, the photographer is on the way, hair and make-up are coming, the caterer and the DJ are ready, etc. *Will all the flower arrangements be done in time? Will the weather stay beautiful? Will it be too hot? Holy cow, these caterpillars are out of control! They're climbing up all the linen tablecloths. Why, oh why, did I suggest we have the wedding at our house? It's okay, Katrina! It's fine! Everything is going to be just fine.*

An alarm goes off on my phone during pre-wedding preparations. The banner on my phone reads, "Check jury message." *Dang it!* I stop for a moment and pull up the website to check the messages. "Panels 1, 2, 3, 9, 10, and 11 report to the courthouse at 9:00 a.m. on Monday, April 11." I stare at the screen to be sure I read it right. I pull out my juror sheet and confirm that I am Panel 11. *Are you kidding me? I don't have time for jury duty on Monday!* I have a wedding to clean up after and I'm way behind on work due to preparing for the wedding. I walk out to the garage where a friend and her mom are feverishly putting together flower arrangements. "You're not going to believe this," I announce. "I have jury duty on Monday."

"You're kidding?!" my friend exclaims, barely looking up from the arrangement she's putting together. "Just what you need right now. It seems like you haven't gotten a break in a long time."

I also take note that they are calling more panels than normal. It must be getting more difficult to get people to show up, or maybe this is a case they think they'll need a bigger pool for. I'm not sure.

I quickly send a text to a judge, who's a friend of mine, letting him know I'd been called for jury duty. "Excellent," he replies. "I'm on that case. I hope you get picked. You will be a perfect juror. You're smart and have some common sense. I'll see you Monday!"

I stick my phone back in my pocket. *Great, no getting out of it now. Sigh, just focus on the wedding, Katrina.*

About then the cinnamon rolls show up in lieu of a wedding cake. My daughter has dealt with a severe egg allergy her entire life as well as a peanut allergy. Until she was twelve or so, she also had a wheat allergy but fortunately "outgrew" that. She was involved in a two-year-long study at the children's hospital for her egg allergy, and although her symptoms have lessened, she still cannot have anything with eggs in it. Before the study, one bite of something with any egg in it would cause an anaphylactic reaction; even cross-contamination could provoke a reaction. Now her symptoms are treatable with Benadryl. So, we've had to get creative for a "cake." There's a baker in town who has made egg-free cupcakes for us, but the recipe really wouldn't work well for a whole cake. We were going to get the cupcakes and use a wood-tiered cupcake holder we'd been given, but instead, my daughter decided on cinnamon rolls from a place she had worked at briefly. They're incredibly good cinnamon rolls, and I'm sure they will go over well. As I walk outside to inspect them, the smell of freshly baked bread with cinnamon wafts through the air. I knew she'd made a good choice. Now to just keep the caterpillars out of them!

It's 5:00 p.m., wedding time! Everything falls into place perfectly. My daughter is stunning, the food is amazing, the cinnamon roll "cake" is all the rage, the flowers and decorations are perfect, the DJ is incredible, and the small, intimate group my daughter wanted is here to share it with her. By 9:00 p.m., she and her husband drive off, and the handful of us who are left begin the cleanup.

My beautiful daughter, married off at twenty-one, to an outstanding young man. She was one I would not have expected this from. The early years were oh-so trying. In addition to her food allergies, she dealt with extreme sensory issues, mainly oral, and didn't eat solid food until she was three. The first several years were filled with endless therapy appointments: speech therapy, physical therapy, occupational therapy, etc. We traveled as far as Colorado to see a speech therapist who dealt with the eating issues. Thankfully, those days are now a distant memory. I breathe in and breathe out. Sometimes you're given the opportunity to witness the beauty from ashes.

> *"...to comfort all who mourn, and provide for those who grieve in Zion—to bestow on them a crown of beauty instead of ashes, the oil of joy instead of mourning, and a garment of praise instead of a spirit of despair..." Isaiah 61:2b-3a NIV*

We've gained a new son!

Sunday, April 10th, 2022

IT'S SUNDAY AND WE *ALWAYS* go to church on Sundays. There's just no way this Sunday. My husband and son must make a seven-hour round-trip to take my son's out-of-state girlfriend back to her family. They leave at 6:30 a.m. I have several vendors showing up to pick up rented items and then we have items to return to vendors. I ask the two boys still at home to come help. As usual, only the exchange student is much help. After shaking out all the table linens and bagging them up, I glance over at him to see his face so swollen that his eyes are nearly shut. "Oh, my goodness! You must be allergic to all this pollen we're stirring up. Go on inside and wash your face. I'll get you some meds." He washes his face, takes the meds, and tries to join me back outside. I refuse and tell him he's inside for the rest of the day. I venture back out to the yard in time for the tent rental guys to show up to take down and load the tent.

My husband finally arrives home. He immediately helps me load tables to take back to the church. After loading the tables and returning them, we load all the chairs, and a few other items, to deliver to the rental vendor. It's a hot day for April, and we work up a sweat. I work into the evening sorting through all that's left, taking pictures of what we're going to sell and posting them on Facebook. My daughter had an old-fashioned telephone at the wedding that was used for guests to leave messages on. I box it up to ship it back to the company so they can create an audio file of all the recorded messages. I post pictures of personal items that were left by guests to see if anyone claims them, and then I take a deep breath and settle into my chair to read for a bit. My routine is to sit and read every evening with my dogs. It's my way to wind down and end the day.

"Come to me, all you who are weary
and burdened, and I will give you rest."
Matthew 11:28 NIV

Monday, April 11th, 2022

I ARRIVE AT THE COURTHOUSE by 9:00 a.m., barely. I'm not good at getting myself ready and out the door at an earlier hour. Although 9:00 a.m. isn't that early, I work from home and am used to taking my time putting myself together in the morning. I may be "working" by 6:30 a.m., but I'm certainly not showered and dressed yet.

I shuffle into the courthouse and climb the stairs to the courtroom as instructed. The building is over a hundred years old; I'm certain there has never been any updating. It carries a bit of an old musty smell, and many of the black and white floor tiles have cracked over the years. There are approximately fifty other individuals there, waiting to be let into the courtroom. When the judge and the attorneys finish their pre-jury-selection process and discussions, they let us into the room, and we all find seats. Then begins the *long* process of weeding through those who have shown up and selecting fourteen people: twelve jurors and two alternates. I've been through this process twice already but haven't been selected to serve. I certainly don't have time to be selected, especially when we're told this is likely to be a four- or five-day trial. The legal system and the way trials work seem interesting though. I've always been interested in this process. Still, I'm not sure that I want that responsibility in my life right now. I settle into one of the pew-style benches and study the high ceilings. They're covered with the intricate tiles you often see in older buildings.

The judge begins by letting us know what the charge is, murder in the first-degree, and makes sure we understand that the defendant is innocent until proven guilty. I'm glad to hear him say that; I've always been a fighter for the underdog. He then goes into other aspects of the case and asks if there's any reason why any of us could not be fair and impartial. At this point, no one raises their hand. I believe being fair and impartial will be an obtainable task for me as well. I've always been good at separating facts from feelings, determining relevant versus irrelevant, and studying a situation. Still, I know this is going to be a tough decision for a jury; at least, I feel like it will be for me.

The judge continues with the voir dire process. This is the process the court goes through to select the jury for a trial; it's supposed to find the best, unbiased, impartial, and fair jury for a particular case. The judge begins by introducing the prosecutors for the State. There are four of them. Then, the judge introduces the defendant and her defense attorney. Everyone is then asked if anyone knows any of them. A few hands go up, relationships are disclosed, and a few potential jurors are dismissed. Next, all the State's witnesses are called. There are many witnesses who all enter the courtroom. Their names are read, and everyone is asked if anyone knows any of them. Again, a few hands go up and relationships are discussed. Last, the defense witnesses are all listed, but they're not present. There are fourteen names read. Various individuals' hands go up, indicating that they know some of the people named.

The judge then tells us the trial may last up to five days and wants to know if there's anyone who would be unable to complete the entire trial. A few hands go up, and more people are dismissed due to their circumstances. The judge continues with endless other questions that may rule people out, like if they or a family member had been involved in a violent crime, received a felony, or are currently or formerly employed with law enforcement in some capacity. More hands are raised and a few more are dismissed.

At this point, it's decided that the people who are left should all be fair and impartial, so everyone's name goes in a box for them to randomly draw twenty-eight names. It's been long enough that I'm tired of sitting and hoping that my name isn't called. But, as the twenty-third name is drawn, I hear "Panel 11, Katrina Robertson." *Dang!* I head over to the jury box as my stomach growls.

It's now time for the prosecutors and the defense attorney to have their turn at the voir dire questioning. The State begins. The State remarks that they must prove the defendant's purpose was to commit the death of her husband, that she *intended* to kill him. The prosecutor asks if anyone had been a part of a jury trial in the past. The State prosecutors also ask if anyone was involved previously in a violent crime or falsely accused of a crime. I sit silently through the whole process since none of it applies to me. The prosecutor then gives instructions to us called "The Commonsense Instruction." The prosecutor states this means you're not to leave your common sense and your affairs in life at the door. "When you come in as a juror, and if you're picked to be on this jury, we want you to use your common sense," she states. "Do not leave your common sense at the door when you're assessing the information." *Now, this instruction I like! I can get behind common sense any day! It seems this has been left behind in so many areas of our culture today.*

I can no longer ignore my hunger pangs, and I try to distract myself by counting the beads on my bracelet. I've never been good at sitting for long periods of time, but the defense still has their turn. The defense attorney starts by talking about himself. He then moves on to say how he wants to hear from each one of us. He asks us to be patient with him while he makes his way to each juror. I was the twenty-third name called, and he is going in order. *Man, I don't want to hear all these other people's life stories.* He finally gets to me. I give him a brief bio and he asks if I've ever served on jury duty. I tell him I've gotten to this "level" before but was never selected. He asks how that makes me feel. I tell him it's a big responsibility that I don't take lightly. He then moves on to the next juror. Finally, he explains the emotional aspects we will face in this trial and says, "As a juror, it's your job to separate emotion from facts." *I like this instruction too. I know I can do this.*

The judge gives us a short break and tells us to be back at 12:45 p.m. when the selected jurors will be called up. *Lunch,* that's all I can think about at this point. But we weren't given enough time for that. I take my bathroom break, get a drink, and head back to the courtroom. I decide I don't want to do this for the rest of the week. As we all take our seats, there seems to be some nervous tension in the air. The court clerk begins reading off the names: Juror #1, Juror #2, etc. As she makes her way through the list, I feel like I may be getting out of it, and then "Juror #11, Katrina Robertson" is announced. I numbly rise and take my seat in the jury box where I'm told to sit. One more juror is named and then two alternates. We all stare out in front of us as if we're the ones who've just been sentenced. The rest of the jurors who were not selected are dismissed. The remaining fourteen of us are given more instructions and then dismissed for lunch. When we return, the trial will begin.

I leave the courthouse and dial my husband's number while heading somewhere to snag a bite to eat. "Give me the good news," he declares as he answers the phone.

"If getting chosen for jury duty for a four or five-day murder trial is good, there's your good news," I reply.

"Oh my gosh, Katrina! I didn't want this on your shoulders right now. I'm so sorry! I'll take up the slack for the rest of the week."

I decide what I need is an energy drink to help me get through the rest of the day in the courtroom. I snag one at a gas station, with a snack, and settle in my car to check my emails, voicemails, and texts. I'm an independent financial adviser and, fortunately, have the flexibility to work from about anywhere. I make a couple of calls, send a few emails, and compile notes of things to do when I'm back at my home office. It's time to head back inside the courthouse. I decide I'm going to have a good attitude about jury duty. This is a huge responsibility and a civic duty. I'm determined to listen closely, take notes, and come to the right decision for the defendant and the victim. Fortunately, the energy drink is kicking in.

All of us jurors are back in our assigned seats on time. I doubt anyone, even if normally late for events, would risk being late for the trial. As the judge enters, we're told to rise, and it's announced that court is in session. The prosecution gets the first turn at opening arguments. I've noticed now that they get to go first for everything.

A prosecutor takes the stand, and it seems to me she's made for TV drama, and we're going to get *all* of it. The prosecutor puts on a show, raises her voice, tells a story, and plays with our emotions. *Wow!* I think. *That's impressive and all, but I hope this whole thing isn't a play on emotions and a made-for-TV drama.* I'm not sure if all four of the State prosecutors introduced during the voir dire questioning are going to be involved in the trial, but now it appears they are. *That doesn't seem fair,* I think to myself. *Why does the State get four people to argue their case and the defendant only one?* The State prosecutor settles down and it's now time for the defense attorney to take the stage.

He isn't nearly as dramatic but still tells a story. The defense attorney paints a picture of a woman who suffers from PTSD and lived in an abusive relationship. He describes a woman who was fifty-seven years old at the time of the crime, was a piano teacher to children, and had never been in trouble. I study the lady sitting at the defense table. She's sixty years old now, but she carries more years than that in her face. *Had this woman really been in an abusive relationship? Had she been pushed beyond what she could bear? Did she really have a right to claim "self-defense" that day she shot her husband?* I hope those questions can be answered "beyond a reasonable doubt" before the trial is over. The defense attorney then states, "You may be wondering why there are four of them and one of me." *Yes, yes, I am!* I answer in my head. "That's because they're the ones with the burden of proof. My client is not guilty. I have nothing to prove. Only the State has something to prove. That's also why they always go first and get to go again when I'm finished." So, I guess that answers my question, but it still doesn't seem fair.

The State gets up for their second opening argument. Another of the prosecutors takes a turn and it's another drama-filled scene. They keep me on the edge of my seat, but, in the end, I'm only interested in facts. I realize their main argument is going to be that the murder victim was disabled and thus unable to abuse the defendant, giving her no right to claim she shot him in self-defense. I'm sure the severity of his disability will be argued about further, but I already know that a disabled person is still able to abuse another individual. Abuse comes in many forms. The victim's disability was physical, but I shudder slightly when I think of the atrocious abuse my "mentally disabled" son could dish out, and often got away with, under the veil of his disability. My anxiety heightens. This is going to be challenging.

I leave the courthouse completely fried. My brain is soup. I cook dinner nearly every night, but tonight I tell my family that they're on their own. I don't have an appetite. I worry about our exchange student. He has Crohn's disease and a very strict diet. I'm always careful in selecting and preparing meals for him, and there are limited options for fast food for him. I must let it go for this week. I sit down to sort through the mail, and a package has come for me. It's a heart monitor. My doctor was concerned about some low blood pressure episodes I'd had and sent me to a cardiologist. I'm sure it's stress-related. All my medical issues seem to circle back to stress. I read the instructions, set the device up, and attach it to my chest. The monitor is a cell phone. I sure don't need that thing going off in court and the bailiff thinking I have a cell phone on me. The instructions say I need to start the monitoring immediately, so I affix it and cross my fingers that it won't cause any issues. I grab my book and head to my chair to read with my dogs. This morning feels like a week ago. I don't get far in my book before I'm ready to call it a night. I'll be having to rely on the Lord to get me through this week.

> *"I can do all this through him who gives me strength." Philippians 4:13 NIV*

Tuesday and Wednesday, April 12ᵗʰ and 13ᵗʰ, 2022

TWO FULL DAYS OF TESTIMONY after testimony after testimony. We're given small notebooks to keep our notes in, but we must leave them in the courtroom. Each time we take breaks, we're not allowed to speak to anyone. When we're sent to the jury room, we can talk to each other, but not about the case. It's challenging to keep the conversation about things like the weather when we're part of a murder trial, but we do. At one point a juror asks, "Is it just me, or do some of you want to raise your hand and be like, 'I have a question'?"

"Oh, my goodness, yes!" I reply. "Like why can't we ask questions? We're the ones who must make this decision, but we can't ask questions of the witnesses? I mean, we're the judges in this case and a judge would be allowed to ask questions." Several of the jurors nod in agreement but it is obvious that we feel like that conversation is probably not an allowed topic, so we go back to the weather.

Most of the witnesses are for the State. I think I counted seventeen witnesses. It's laborious listening to that many people say the same thing over and over and over. It seems like overkill on the part of the State but, as the defense attorney said, I guess they're trying to prove their point.

There are fourteen witnesses named for the defendant but, when it is the defense's turn to call witnesses, one by one, the State objects to them. The defense would call them, the State would object, the counsel would approach the bench, and then the judge would allow the objection. At one point, the judge sends us back to the jury room so they can argue more freely over whether a particular witness could speak. In the end, I believe three witnesses speak for the defense, and then the defendant herself speaks.

When the defendant is cross-examined by the State, it's a painful scene to watch. The prosecutors yell at her, cut her off, ridicule her, seem to harass her, push her buttons, and then chuckle when the crazy person they want to emerge does. It seems at times that the defense attorney could object to their treatment of her, but he doesn't. I'm not sure why.

Maybe so we could see some of the "PTSD" come out, the erratic behavior of someone under stress? I'm glad when it finishes, and I wonder if any of the other jurors have the same perspective I do of the whole scene.

It's the end of Day Three, and both sides "rest" their case. All that's left are the final arguments and for us, the jury, to deliberate. The judge decides it's a good time to pause the trial and start again tomorrow. I can tell the jury is glad. None of us want to stay into the night hours.

I go home mentally and emotionally drained. *Why were most of the defense witnesses not allowed to speak? What would their testimony have been? Could they have been there to testify about the abuse in the relationship?* I have no way of knowing. I am a top-down learner. I am a big-picture kind of person. However unorthodox it may be, I need to see the full picture of a situation to best discern it. During voir dire, both sides had talked about needing all the pieces of a puzzle to determine what the picture was, and I don't feel like I have all the pieces of the puzzle. I feel stuck and trapped.

It was stressed during the trial to not research "the case." We were instructed to not look up anything on "the case" or talk to anyone about "the case." I don't have a problem with this. I'm confident I have more information about "the case" than anywhere I could go to research or talk about it. What I don't know much about is the victim; we were only told that he was disabled. *Possibly an alcoholic?* His daughter had testified, but she testified she hadn't seen her father in a few years. I know the State's biggest argument against the defendant's right to claim "self-defense" from abuse is that the victim was disabled. It is true he often used a wheelchair due to a stroke a couple of years before his death at the defendant's hands, but I also remember hearing testimony that he could walk. Then I remember being told I couldn't research the parties of the case. *Hmmm, is the victim really a "party" to the case?* I mean, he wasn't present for the hearing nor was he part of the voir dire questioning. I feel like I have found my loophole. My fingers dance across my keyboard to type his name into a public records database. *Wait,* I think. *What if I find incriminating evidence against him? What if I find factual records that he's abusive or an alcoholic? Surely, if they're out there, the defense would have brought them up. But what if that information isn't allowed for some reason? Why wouldn't it be? It's certainly relevant.* I remember, "Don't leave your common sense at the door." I have full confidence in myself that I can successfully separate any information I find from the facts presented during the case. I continue with my search. Nothing. That's what I find. Absolutely nothing. I close my computer and head to my chair to read. I whisper a silent prayer that God would give me wisdom, discernment, and strength for tomorrow.

> *"If any of you lacks wisdom, you should ask God, who gives generously to all without finding fault, and it will be given to you."*
> *James 1:5 NIV*

Thursday, April 14th, 2022

I GET UP A LITTLE earlier than normal so I can have an extra strong cup of coffee and get my mind right. I listen to some music that helps me "put my game face on" and text some close friends, asking them to send up some prayers for me. I head to the courthouse and meet up with the other jurors in the jury room. We sit quietly as we wait for the judge to call us in for the closing arguments. I am certain that most of us are well situated with how we stand with the case. The bailiff sticks his head in the room, "Y'all ready?" Obviously, it doesn't matter if we're ready or not. We shuffle, single file, out to the courtroom. Most of the jurors grab jackets as they walk out of the jury room. They complain the courtroom is like a freezer. I don't notice this. I sweat when I'm anxious, and I've been sweating plenty the past few days. I pass the victim's daughter and make eye contact with her. My heart goes out to her, and her whole family. Regardless of how distant they had become with their father, whatever struggles they may have had, I have no doubt they have been through a nightmare.

We all take our assigned seats, and the State stands to begin their closing arguments. If I had thought their opening arguments were drama-filled and "made-for-TV," I'm not prepared for their closing arguments. I had seen courtroom drama played out on TV shows. I hadn't realized until now that they put on these seemingly rehearsed, dramatic monologues in real life. I must admit, she's good, really good. Even through all the production, however, I remember what was said earlier in the week. I'm here for facts, not emotion. After the State prosecutor works up a sweat, she sits down. The defense attorney stands for his turn. He also turns up the show, but not nearly to the level of the State. He tells the story again: the defendant's action was justifiable self-defense. Nothing more, nothing less.

Just like the opening arguments, the State gets a second closing argument and a chance at the final word. The State prosecutor rises and begins her monologue as she saunters to the podium. She then pulls out a blown-up picture of the autopsied body of the victim, an item that had been admitted as evidence. She displays it in front of the jury and continues her argument. I roll my eyes at this antic. Again, it's a simple emotional manipulation maneuver by the State. *He's dead. We get it. Is displaying his dead body necessary?* I'm beyond thankful when she finishes. I'm certain my facial expressions can no longer hide my thoughts.

The judge then begins to give us our instructions. He reads them to us, word-for-word, from a binder that he says he will provide to us when we head to deliberate. Part of the instruction is that we are to "accept without question [his] rulings as to the admissibility or rejection of evidence." I think about the witnesses that weren't allowed to speak. I guess witnesses are, on some level, a type of "evidence". Shouldn't it have been determined *before* the trial if their testimony shouldn't be allowed though? The judge continues through the instructions. He states, "You are the sole judges of the weight of the evidence and the credibility of the witnesses. In determining the credibility of any witness and the weight to be given his testimony, you may take into consideration his demeanor while on the witness stand, any prejudice for or against a party, his means of acquiring knowledge concerning any matter to which he testified, any interest he may have in the outcome of the case, the consistency or inconsistency or his testimony, it's reasonableness or unreasonableness, and any other fact or circumstance tending to shed light upon the truth or falsity of his testimony." *But we weren't allowed to be the sole judges of all the witnesses.* I think to myself. I had the opportunity to "judge" all the witnesses for the prosecution, but not the defense. *I really don't like this position I've been put in.* If I could recuse myself, I would probably consider it, but both our alternate jurors have already been utilized.

He continues with more information about evidence, the burden of proof, the presumption of innocence, and what reasonable doubt is. He reminds us that the charge is first-degree murder and reads the statute that must be satisfied before the defendant can be found guilty. The main requirement of the first-degree murder charge is the defendant's intent to kill the victim. He explains that we must first decide if the defendant is guilty or not guilty of that charge, unanimously. If we decide unanimously that she's not guilty, then we move to the lesser charge of second-degree murder. If she's not guilty of that, we move to the next lesser charge of manslaughter, and so forth. He explains the requirements of each statute to us in a concise manner. Then there's a second charge against the defendant: a felony firearm enhancement. If you kill someone with a gun, there can be a second charge added on top of the murder charge. This makes no sense to me. *So, if she beat him to death with a bat, there isn't an "enhancement" that can be added for that? Or what about a knife? Everyone is okay with that too?* I guess we get to sort that out during deliberations. The judge finishes giving his instructions. The court is now in recess. We retire to the jury room. We aren't allowed to leave at this point, so the bailiff takes our lunch orders.

We all stare at each other, not sure how to start. After three full days of not being allowed to speak about the case, now we're supposed to talk about the case. We simply don't know how to proceed. We decide that we will wait till our lunch arrives, eat, and then begin our deliberations. We elect Juror #5 as our foreman. He seems to be a good choice, and he accepts the responsibility.

We finish our meal and begin an unorganized round of discussion and questions. We discuss various pieces of evidence that were admitted, pull out a diagram of the crime scene, and decide we need to see a police camera video again. The video is in the courtroom, so we get a message to the bailiff that we want to see a video again. The foreman then tries to bring some organization to our discussion and sets some ground rules. We needed that. I suggest we take a preliminary vote just to see where we are right now and how much deliberating we need to do. He agrees, and we decide to go around the table and share if we believe she's guilty or not guilty of first-degree murder. Nine jurors vote "guilty" and three, including myself, vote "not guilty" on the first-degree murder charge. I'm surprised and I can tell Juror #2, sitting across from me, is as well.

"Wait!" I exclaim. "The main thing that must be proven for first-degree murder is that she *wanted* to kill her husband. That she *intended* to kill him. The prosecution had *seventeen* witnesses testify and not *one* of them proved this. They simply proved that she killed him, not that she *meant* to kill him that day. The entire prosecution's side was built to play on and manipulate our emotions. It was a dog-and-pony show." My emotions begin to get the best of me, and the tears start to fall. The deliberations continue, and I'm struggling. It may be cold in the courtroom, but the jury room is hot and stuffy. Another jury member opens a side door to a private room to see if that helps get more air circulating.

Juror #10, who is sitting next to me, proposes, "Why don't we take a break?" Everyone agrees, and I know it's because they're hoping I can pull myself together. He nods toward the private room that's behind the door that had been opened and suggests I take a minute to myself in there. I decline and take a bathroom break.

I return from the bathroom, but the weight is even heavier on my shoulders. The responsibility of determining another human being's guilt or innocence is overwhelming to me. *Am I the only one?* Several jurors are back to discussing sports scores and the weather while I'm trying to process that what we decide in this room will determine another person's future. We *must* get this vote right. "I'm ready to proceed."

The tears begin to fall again, and I stutter, "You guys are just going to have to deal with the tears; they aren't going to stop."

The foreman speaks up, "We will take as long as we need to. This is important. We want to be sure we aren't trying to persuade someone in a direction they don't believe is the right way." Everyone nods their heads in agreement.

"I have a disabled son," I start. "I have experienced unspeakable trauma by him." My heart begins to beat faster, and I catch my breath. I steady my breathing to continue. "If one of the times he was trying to come at me, and I saw a gun, I could see myself shooting my son, you guys. I don't know about y'all, but all these unanswered questions about the defense's witnesses not being able to speak got the best of me last night. I looked the victim up on Court Connect just to see if he had any criminal records. There was nothing there. Nothing at all. We have no evidence at all that he was abusive other than the defendant's testimony. There was no evidence entered in court. I respect the Court and must believe there were valid reasons those testimonies weren't allowed. We only have her testimony. I believe her testimony. My gut believes she suffered PTSD and she genuinely felt in danger at that moment. I'm forced to examine only the facts of the case. I'm to investigate only what was presented in that courtroom. I'm sorry guys. I'm just struggling." I can tell many of them have empathy for me at that moment. I continue, "We were told we would all bring our own life experiences and perspectives into the jury room. I'm just being honest with mine." They all nod and I realize that in the hundreds of questions asked during voir dire, "Have you ever been abused by a disabled person?" wasn't one of them. I wonder if it should have been. Would a "yes" to that question have made me more, or less, valuable to this trial?

We all decide to vote again: unanimously not guilty of first-degree murder. I'm a little stunned. How do the majority of them so easily and quickly change their vote? A couple of jurors admit that they cannot declare "guilty beyond a reasonable doubt." Sometime around this point, the bailiff announces that the video is now ready for us to view. We'd forgotten we had requested it and had moved on from that. We start to tell him "never mind" but realize they've had to call *everyone* back to the courtroom for us to view it. None of us understand why everyone has to be present for us to view the video again, but we now feel obligated to go ahead and head back out to the courtroom to view it. We watch it, thank them, and go back to the jury room.

Our foreman gets us organized again. Since we've decided the defendant is not guilty of first-degree murder, we must now move to second-degree. He reads aloud the statute outlining the criteria for a second-degree murder charge. There are a few bullet points, but the one that we all stop on is "a reckless disregard for human life." We pull the crime scene back out, we study the layout—where the body was found, as well as the gun—and we discuss the order of events according to the testimonies given. Did she have other options? Was her life *really* in danger? We discuss it thoroughly. We decide it's time to vote. We go around the room. It comes to me; I close my eyes and whisper, "Guilty." It's unanimous.

I hadn't realized until this moment how difficult it would be to utter the word "guilty" regarding another human being. Is it so agonizing because the facts presented in the trial lead me to a verdict that my emotions don't want to go with? Is it just that I don't feel equipped to judge another human being? I'm not sure, but I do know I never want to be put in the same situation again.

It is now time for us to determine sentencing. The maximum sentence for second-degree murder is thirty years, but there is also the felony firearm enhancement, which carries a maximum of ten years. So, we're looking at a maximum of forty years, and we decide to start by just going around the room and commenting on how many years we think are appropriate, in total. Our answers vary. There is also the option for fines. We eliminate the fines quickly. We discuss the "truth in sentencing" concept the State had explained to make us aware that when someone is sentenced to a certain number of years, they're never going to actually serve that many years. You could anticipate cutting the sentence in half right off the bat and then cutting it in half again if the person shows good behavior.

Several of the jurors had voted for a maximum sentence in the first vote we took. I speak up, "You guys realize that the reason no one serves their given sentence is that there's simply no space in jails to keep these people locked up, right? I'm not saying that the taking of someone's life doesn't deserve punishment, but let's remember the reality here. We have a sixty-year-old woman who hasn't been in any other serious trouble. She is not a true danger to society. She is now going to have a felony on her record. Life for her is going to be much more arduous *out* of prison now. Do we need to be taking up prison bed space with her when there are much more dangerous people on the streets that keep getting let out?"

"But what about the victim's family?" a juror asks. "Don't they deserve justice for the murder of their family member?"

"No amount of jail time or fine can satisfy the value of a life taken," I respond. "This is something his family is going to have to work through. Forgiveness will be huge."

There isn't much more discussion after this. We decide we will go around the room, take down everyone's vote, then average the votes. We start to my left. Twenty years, twenty years, twenty years, etc. It's obvious everyone is going straight down the middle. Then we get to Juror #8, two people to my right. Juror #8 proudly states, "Forty years!" I sigh. She had been one of the most reluctant to come down off the first-degree murder charge. I believe she wants the defendant hung. Two more votes, both twenty years. I'm the last one to go. "Zero," I say simply to bring Juror #8's vote for the maximum of forty back down to twenty, the middle ground which is the consensus of everyone else. It earns me an eye roll from Juror #8.

We now allocate the twenty years between the two charges. We decide on seventeen for second-degree murder and three for the felony firearm enhancement. We all agree that the firearm enhancement is silly and almost allocate twenty to second-degree murder and zero to it but are afraid that would draw questions, and, at the end of the day, it doesn't matter. It's time to let the bailiff know we have reached a verdict and sentence.

Now we have the awkward interval in the jury room while we wait for everyone to gather back in the courtroom. We share nervous chatter while we wait. "I'm going to ask the judge when this is all over about why there were objections to so many of the defense's witnesses and why we couldn't know what their testimony was and why it wasn't allowed," I say.

"You know the judge?" another juror asks.

"I do," I respond, "and I feel like he'll also tell me if we were on the same page he would have been on with the verdict and the sentencing."

"Cool," another juror responds, "I'd like to have feedback as well."

One of the other female jurors begins talking. "I just can't believe she [referring to the defendant] hasn't been in jail this whole time. I walked past her in the parking lot the other day!" She said it as though the defendant were an untouchable, a lesser-than, someone who should not be sharing the same space as her. I stare in her direction, tilt my head, and slant my eyes. I decide I won't speak my thoughts, but I'm sure my facial expression speaks for itself. *Am I the weird one here who sees this lady as simply another human being instead of just a "murderer"?*

"Y'all ready?" The bailiff asks as he sticks his head in the door. We all take a deep breath and line up to head into the courtroom. I pass by the victim's daughter, and I try to catch her eye and somehow transmit a virtual hug to her. I know this is not going to be the verdict and sentencing she is wishing for or what she believes her father deserves. I take my seat and peer across the courtroom at the defendant. She sips water nervously. I'm too far away to catch her eye. I know this won't be the verdict she's hoping for, either.

"All rise," the bailiff announces as the judge enters the courtroom. "Court is now in session."

The judge adjusts his glasses and shuffles the papers in front of him. "The jury has reached their verdict and sentencing. For the charge of first-degree murder, the jury finds the defendant not guilty. For the charge of second-degree murder, the jury finds the defendant guilty. For the felony firearm enhancement, the jury finds the defendant guilty."

I watch the defendant. No reaction. "The jury has assessed a seventeen-year sentence on the charge of second-degree murder and added a three-year sentence on the firearm enhancement, for a total of twenty years." The judge then addresses the jury. "And who was appointed as the foreman for the jury?"

Juror #5 raises his hand.

"And this is your signature on these forms?"

"Yes, sir," answers Juror #5.

The judge then starts with Juror #1 and goes down the line to each jury member to verify that this is the verdict and sentencing that we agreed to. We all confirm that, yes, that's how each of us voted.

"Very well," responds the judge. He then gives some additional instructions, but I've zoned out by this point.

The bailiff comes over to us and instructs us that we're to leave behind all the notes we took, along with the jury pin we've each been wearing, and that he will escort us out to the parking lot. He also returns our phones that we had turned in at the start of the day. We find our way to the front door. I walk out with Juror #2 and #10. Juror #2 raises both hands. "It's so amazing to be in the sunshine and be free!" he exclaims.

I'm in such a daze that I forget for a moment where I had parked. I find my car, roll down the windows, and start it up to get it cooled off. I take a moment to glance at my phone. It's chock-full of emails, texts, voicemails, etc. The weight of the past four days hits me, and the emotions come. I need a moment before I can drive home. I text my husband, "We're done, but I need a minute."

"Take your time. I'll figure dinner out," he responds.

I sit for thirty minutes or so. This is one of those experiences that I don't respond to exactly how I would have previously expected before arriving at this moment. I'm a strong person, a passionate person; I speak my mind, and I die on hills. This leaves me completely and utterly worn out. I'm not sure of all the reasons for that. Maybe it's the culmination of all the other stress in my life? I'm not sure. "Take a breath, Katrina; it's over," I whisper to myself. I text a friend and let her know I'm finished. She knows what a toll this has taken on me and invites me to dinner later that evening. I take her up on the offer and head home.

I arrive at home where my husband and boys are dishing out dinner from some place's takeout containers. I give my husband a summary of the verdict and sentencing we arrived at and tell him a friend is picking me up for dinner. The emotions well up in me again, and he gives me a hug and kiss on the forehead. "I'll be all right," I utter. "That was just … a lot."

My friend picks me up at my place and we head to our most common spot for cheese dip and drinks. We never actually have a meal, and I certainly don't have the appetite for one. I pour out all the details of the case I've been holding in, my frustrations, and the emotional toll it has taken on me. "I wanted to look up records on every one of the witnesses, the defendant, find them on Facebook and scroll their pages—even the defense attorney. I'm not sure about him and the tactics he was using."

"As you should!" she responds. "You had a big responsibility and should have access to all information."

"Yeah, well, apparently that's not the case. I do plan on reaching out to the defense attorney. We went to the same college at about the same time. I would love to talk to him about what in the world was going on behind the scenes. Apparently, as a juror, your job is to sit down, shut up, follow instructions, don't ask any questions or question anything, keep it easy, and go with group think. I'm not that girl. Anyway, I'm glad it's over, and I do feel at peace with the verdict we reached, even if it wasn't what my heart wanted; I just have more questions I'd like answered."

We finish up the last of our cheese dip and drinks and decide it's time to head home. She brings me home and reaches across the vehicle console for a hug. "Love you, friend. Get some rest," she encourages.

"Love you too. Thanks for the drinks and cheese dip." I head inside, change my clothes, wash my face, brush my teeth, and sit down in my chair. My mind is still not in a place to read, so I pick up my phone and start checking notifications.

I find the defense attorney on Facebook, send him a friend request, and shoot him a quick message. "Hey, I was a juror on the trial that just wrapped up and I would love to get together with you to talk about some of the questions I had during the trial. You sure didn't have much to work with!"

I then shoot the judge a text. "That was one of the most excruciating processes I've ever been through. I have so many questions. I will have to pick your brain at some point."

The judge responds fairly quickly. "Now you know why I love to have juries decide cases instead of me. It's hard. I want to pick your brain asap as well to see how I can do a better job with juries. How do you look for next week? I'll buy."

"I can make most any day work except Friday. Tuesday, I have a 1:00, so I'd have to be done in time for that."

"Let me look at my calendar for next week. It's busy but meeting with you is very important to me. I'll make something work. I'll text you later tonight. Are you exhausted?"

"*Very* exhausted. My mind is still racing, so I don't see going to sleep soon or sleeping well."

"So how do you like being the judge?"

"*Hate* it! I seriously nearly had a breakdown having to say the word 'guilty.' Let's do lunch."

"Agreed. I'll get with you next week."

I close the apps on my phone and head to bed.

"Therefore, my child, be strengthened in the grace that is in Christ Jesus." 2 Timothy 2:1 ASV

Monday, April 18th, 2022

THE DEFENSE ATTORNEY ACCEPTS MY friend request and responds to my message. "I would love to get together with you and discuss the case. However, there are reasons I can't speak with you right now."
Hmmm, okay then.

Tuesday, April 19th, 2022

I REALIZE THE JUDGE HASN'T gotten back to me on when he is available for lunch, so I shoot him a quick text. "No time for lunch this week?" I ask.

The whole day goes by. No response. It's not like him, but I know he's busy. I feel like I'm recovering from the trial and decide I'll probably never have good answers to those questions, and it'll be okay.

> *"For God is not a God of confusion but of peace."* 1 Corinthians 14:33a ESV

Wednesday, April 20th, 2022

I HAVE AN APPOINTMENT WITH my tattoo artist. Yes, this Christian, pastor's wife, and professional financial advisor has a tattoo artist. I want to get "Be Still" with Exodus 14:14 put on my left forearm.

I've been a fighter for years now. Mainly fighting for others. Fighting for my kids. I'm worn out and I feel like God is telling me it's time to "be still" for a while. This will be a tough thing for me to do, and I know I will need the constant reminder.

I share my jury duty story with the artist. I've been in his room many times. He's perplexed by some of what I share and scratches his head. "That just doesn't make sense," he remarks.

"Yeah, I know. Maybe one day it will make sense."

He finishes up, and I admire the finished product. It's just what I wanted.

"The Lord will fight for you; you need only to be still." Exodus 14:14 NIV

Tuesday, April 26th, 2022

I'M WORKING AT MY COMPUTER when an email comes across from the court with an attachment. I open it up and my heart skips a beat. It's a summons to appear in court on May

11th. The defense is citing juror misconduct and asking for a motion for a new trial. My mind starts racing. *What in the world?!* I catch my breath. *What's happening?! I thought this was over! What kind of juror misconduct could justify the defense wanting a new trial?* I shoot texts to a few people and begin pacing. *This must be something about me,* I think. That's got to be why the judge and the defense attorney won't speak to me. I send my theory to a friend. "I think it's me. I think it's something I did wrong!"

"Calm down. You're being ridiculous. You don't know that."

Two weeks and a day. That's how long I must dwell on this. It feels like an eternity. A friend reaches out, asking how she can help. *How in the world can she help this?* Then it comes to me how she can help. She's good with words and I have *no* words now. I don't feel like I can form a complete sentence. "I want to come prepared to court with an apology. If this is all about me, I'm worried I won't be able to find my words, and I want something written down. Can you help me write something out?"

"Absolutely," she responds.

> *"Do not be anxious about anything, but in every situation, by prayer and petition, with thanksgiving, present your requests to God. And the peace of God, which transcends all understanding, will guard your hearts and your minds in Christ Jesus." Philippians 4:6-7 NIV*

Wednesday, April 27th, 2022

I DECIDE IT'S SAFE NOW to go ahead and research this defense attorney. I can't focus on anything else anyway, and research is something I'm good at. I begin going through public records, newspaper articles, and testimonies, and what I find appalls me. The defense attorney has a criminal record himself and has even had his law license suspended at one time due to the charges. I don't believe he can be trusted. *Why would he even be asking for a retrial? Does he not realize that, unless he has new evidence or testimony, he very well may be giving his client a worse verdict and sentencing? Why is he doing this?* I shoot a Facebook message to a friend to share my thoughts.

> *"Do not be afraid of them; the LORD your God himself will fight for you."*
> *Deuteronomy 3:22 NIV*

Tuesday, May 10th, 2022

I'M TRYING TO READ IN my chair and relax. It's not working. The tears keep falling. My husband sits down on the couch across from me. "I'm scared. Why is this happening?" I ask him.

"Take a peek at your arm." I rub the words "Be Still" and continue to cry. "The Lord's going to fight for you," he says.

The tears keep falling as I twist the wet tissue in my hand. I can't really talk, so I grab another tissue and pet the dog in my lap.

My view many evenings.

"My flesh and my heart may fail, but God is the strength of my heart and my portion forever." Psalm 73:26 NIV

Wednesday, May 11ᵗʰ, 2022

I WAKE IN THE MORNING and open my Facebook messages. My friend, the one I had messaged with my concerns about the defendant getting a worse verdict and sentencing if a mistrial is granted, had never continued the conversation. I now realize I had sent that message to the defense attorney, not the friend I intended. *Good grief.* My brain hasn't been working. *No big deal, he needs to know that.* I delete the message anyway and block him.

The past two weeks have been a blur for me. I've tried to busy myself with my work and household responsibilities, but I've just been going through the motions. Court is at 1:30 p.m. today, and I arrive a little early. We head upstairs and are directed to a different courtroom than the one where the trial had been held. This is a different judge. My heart speeds up. The original judge has recused himself.

I'm herded to the jury room with all the other jurors. All parties from the trial are in the courtroom, including the victim's family, the defendant's family, and some witnesses. A bailiff confirms we have no phones and instructs us that there's to be no speaking at all. He stays present in the room to ensure that we don't speak. He tells us we will be called out one-by-one to testify.

The hearing is audibly getting started in the courtroom, but we in the jury room can't make out any specific words. A bailiff then sticks his head in and calls for Juror #1. Time passes, she doesn't return, then they ask for Juror #2, and so forth. Juror #10 has been excused due to a medical procedure, and then they skip me and go to Juror #12. I'm left sitting alone in the jury room. *Yep, this is about me, and they've saved me for last.* I reach into my purse and pull out something to take for anxiety. My hands are shaking while sweat rolls down my back. I have to take slow, deep breaths. The door opens again: "Katrina Robertson." I shuffle into the courtroom, take a seat on the stand, and adjust the microphone.

The defense attorney starts the questioning.

Q: Would you please state your name for the record?
A: Katrina Robertson.
Q: And Ms. Robertson, do you recall serving as a
    juror in the State of Arkansas in this trial?
A: I do.

Q: And do you recall your juror number?

A: Eleven.

Q: Ms. Robertson, do you recall being given specific jury instructions from the Court?

A: Yes.

Q: Okay. Do you recall being instructed that outside research and outside information weren't to be made part of the deliberations?

A: Yes.

Q: Ms. Robertson, did you in fact do any independent research or outside research?

A: I did.

Q: What specifically did you research?

A: I simply just looked to see if there was a prior history on the victim.

Q: And what source did you use to research prior history of the victim?

A: Public records.

Q: Okay. Are you familiar with something referred to as Court Connect?

A: Yes.

Q: Did you make statements inside the jury room that you had done independent research?

A: Yes, "Nothing's there."

Q: Did you make a statement in deliberations that you knew you had broken the rules?

A: Not that I recall.

Q: After the trial had concluded, did you in fact add me as a friend on Facebook?

A: Yes, I did.

Q: And for clarity's sake and for transparency, you had no communication with me prior to that, is that correct?

A: No, absolutely not.

Q: And you made statements to me regarding what you've testified to, is that correct?

A: I think I just said, "I'd love to have coffee sometime and discuss the case."

Q: And, in fact, I did not discuss the case with you?

A: No, you did not, and you stated that there was a reason you could not, and obviously, now we know why.

Q: Okay. And you and I have had no further communication since that point, is that correct?

A: That's correct.

Q: Although this morning you did go back into Facebook Messenger and deleted some of the texts that you had sent to me, is that correct?

A: That's because it was meant for somebody else. And texts, plural, would be incorrect.

"Pass the witness," the defense attorney states.

One of the State's prosecutors stands and begins asking me the next round of questions.

Q: Did you make a statement to the other jurors, "Am I the only one that didn't follow the rules?"

A: It's possible? I don't recall though.

Q: Okay. Did you represent to the other jurors— did you tell them that you know the judge?

A: Yes, I did.

Q: And what did you say to them?

A: I said, the judge is a friend of mine and I'm looking forward to speaking with him after all this is done.

Q: Is that all you said about him?

> A: Yes.
> Q: So, you didn't speak with any parties, the defense attorney, during the trial?
> A: No. I didn't even send him a Facebook message till after the trial was over.
> Q: And you didn't communicate with the prosecutors throughout the trial?
> A: No.
> Q: And you didn't communicate with the judge throughout the trial?
> A: No, absolutely not.

"Pass the witness," the prosecutor says.

It goes back to the defense attorney to continue his questioning.

> Q: Ms. Robertson, are you employed in the capacity of a financial advisor?
> A: I am.
> Q: Is the judge one of your clients?

My mouth goes dry and my tongue sticks to the roof of my mouth. *How in the world does he know this?! That's confidential information and irrelevant to me being a juror in his courtroom.* I have no choice but to answer.

> A: He is.
> Q: Okay. And do you work directly with him in advising him or handling financial affairs?
> A: Yes, I do.
> Q: And you recall the voir dire or the questions that were asked before the beginning of the trial?
> A: Yes.

Q: And you recall being asked if you knew or had relationships with any of the participants in the proceedings?

A: The participants that it pertains to are the defense, the prosecution, and the attorneys thereof. The judge is an unbiased individual and whether or not you're friends with him or even a family member with him, is irrelevant.

Q: So, you made that determination and withheld that information during the questions in voir dire?

A: Because during that process it was never asked if anybody knew the judge.

Q: But you admit that you were asked if you knew or had a relationship with any of the participants in the courtroom?

A: That wasn't one of the questions. The question was if you knew any of the, well those with the prosecutors or those with the defense. The judge himself was asking that question.

Q: And at no point in time—I just want to be clear, you never volunteered this relationship with the judge at any point in time?

A: There was no reason to.

I can't wrap my mind around why they are making this such a big deal. I am almost certain even family members of the judge have served on jury duty in his court before. This particular judge is a very well-known and respected individual in our community. They would never be able to put together a jury if they had to eliminate anyone who knew him, or even had dealings with him.

"Pass the witness," the defense attorney states.

Another State prosecutor gets up to continue the questioning.

> Q: If your relationship with the judge is irrelevant, why did you feel the need to tell the other jurors about it?
>
> A: Because I just wanted to say how much I just—there were lots of things left up in the air and questions we all had and I said, "You know, I'm friends with him and I know that he'll go to lunch with me and be able to give me insight to parts of the whole trial system that we as jurors don't understand."

She decides that's all she has to ask. "Pass the witness," she says.

At this point, the judge begins with her questions.

> The Court: So, Ms. Robertson, when you did that, you knew that you were violating the Court's order to you?
>
> A: When I did?
>
> The Court: When you spoke to—when you went on Court Connect and got this information and brought that extraneous information into the jury's deliberations?
>
> A: You know, could I…
>
> The Court: Just a yes or no, ma'am. Did you know that you were violating the Court's order to you?
>
> A: There's a fine line there. I guess, yes?

The problem is I'm overanalyzing the question. I didn't know then, but I obviously know now. I'd like to explain but the judge won't let me do anything but say "yes" or "no."

The Court: You knew. Did you ever think about what that might mean to this trial?

A: Uhm… if I may…

The Court: Just, did you think about what that might mean?

A: Absolutely.

The Court: But you did it anyway?

A: Uhm, if I may, I prepared a statement.

The Court: No, ma'am, I'm asking you questions. That's your role right now is to answer questions.

A: Yes, ma'am.

The Court: So, you didn't think about the bigger picture, about somebody's criminal trial, about people?

A: I did.

The Court: Just a minute. People being called four days in a row to trial, innocent people having to sit there and listen to all this, that might go away because of what you did?

I can't answer her for a long minute. I gaze out at the audience. *Why won't she just let me read what I've written so I can apologize? Why will she not allow me to speak? I didn't realize I was showing up to my own trial here.* I finally manage to speak as the tears begin to fall.

A: It has tormented my soul.

The Court: All right, you may step down. Have a seat with your fellow jurors over there if you don't mind.

I look up, through blurry eyes, and see two jurors sitting there. I guess the others have been dismissed for some reason.

One of the jurors is Juror #8, and then it hits me. *This is because of her! She filed some sort of complaint against me.* I take my seat at the opposite end of the bench from her. I glance in her direction, but she averts her face. *What in the world have you done?* I want to ask her. The fact that I know the judge is completely irrelevant, and that one statement I made in the jury room wasn't even part of our deliberations nor had any effect on the votes. I'm reeling.

The defense attorney then brings an attack against me as he fights for a retrial in a more feverish manner than he even fought for his own client in the original trial. I sit there, listening, dumbfounded. He has brought in numerous witnesses, all to try and prove that my statement would have caused prejudice against his client. The judge turns down his requests for any of them to speak. She decides none of it would be relevant. The defense attorney states that my statement didn't need to have caused prejudice toward his client: what matters is just that it *could* have. I'm trying to wrap my mind around this.

The defense attorney then jumps to the second issue or problem he believes I've created that should give his client a new trial: my relationship with the judge in the first trial. He even uses the fact that the judge has recused himself as evidence that this is a big deal. This is ridiculous to me because I seem to be the one on trial now, not his client, so, of course, it wouldn't make sense to have a judge who knows me making this decision. The defense attorney insists that I lied during voir dire by failing to disclose my relationship with the judge.

The State then gets up to make their arguments against declaring a mistrial:

> I would argue to this Court that based
> on the law in Arkansas that generally,

it's misconduct for a juror to seek out
reading material without the knowledge
of the Court and the parties. Prejudice
doesn't always occur in every case. Rather,
Courts have observed that a defendant is
entitled to a fair trial, not a perfect trial.
And the State cites that exact holding
from Arkansas Courts in its written brief
from *Finch v. State and State v. Cherry.* So
that's the law that we're dealing with here.
Not just whether there was misconduct,
but whether that misconduct actually
prejudiced the defendant and the
Courts have held that prejudice doesn't
automatically occur in every case.

The State then proceeds to argue that my knowing the
judge is not misconduct and should not warrant a mistrial.

The State then addresses the research I did:

But as to the extraneous information
that we heard testimony about today, the
question isn't if that was just misconduct
but also whether that misconduct and
information reached the other jurors
in this case, so I think it's important to
lay out what we heard from these jurors
today:

Juror #1 didn't recall hearing anything
that amounted to misconduct.
Juror #2 didn't recall hearing anything
that amounted to misconduct.

Juror #3 thinks there may have been outside info that was brought in but doesn't remember what it was, maybe that it was said the defendant is crazy.

Juror #4 recalls that something was said about research being done but can't remember what it was. Believes this person did research because of personal experiences with similarities in the trial. There were no physical, tangible documents, printouts, or anything like that.

Juror #5 said he thinks Juror #11 Googled something but wasn't sure what she Googled.

Juror #6 didn't hear of anything that amounted to misconduct.

Juror #7 said that Juror #11 said she didn't find any records on the victim.

Juror #8 said that Juror #11 researched the victim and stated she didn't find any records.

And Juror #9 and Juror #12 both didn't hear any statements that amounted to misconduct.

So that means that out of these jurors testifying today, most of them don't even recall outside information being brought in.

The State continues their argument with mostly unimportant details before concluding with:

To assess whether the defendant was prejudiced or not, the Court, as the defense has stated, doesn't have to understand why this would have been prejudicial according to the defense argument. However, the fact that specific incidences of conduct were kept out by the trial Court doesn't amount to this defendant being prejudiced by Juror #11's actions.

The testimony at trial was that there was an abusive relationship generally. As this Court has sort of determined in speaking with the defense counsel, there were no instances, there were no acts, there were no specific fights testified to. He argues that because Juror 11 went out and found no criminal history, the entire jury panel must have concluded that what the defendant said cannot be true. And that is the only grounds that the defense is moving for this motion on, asserting that the jury found the defendant to be not credible based on this lack of arrest record. And so, because not only did not even half of the jury even hear this information but there's also no reason that this information would have impacted the credibility of the defendant's testimony, there are no grounds to believe that this extraneous information was prejudicial.

And additionally, Your Honor, the State would argue that because the defendant was charged with murder in the first-degree, a class Y felony with the punishment of ten to forty years or life imprisonment, the fact that the jury in this matter sentenced the defendant to murder in the second-degree and sentenced her to seventeen years imprisonment on that charge more so goes to weigh in the fact that this jury did, in fact, believe some of her testimony that she gave on the stand or else they would not have convicted her of such a lesser offense.

At this point, my head is spinning, and the defense attorney stands to make another argument. He is more animated now and jumps back on my relationship with the judge and how important it is that I should have disclosed that. He goes on and on and on about how this alone gives cause for a new trial. After several minutes he then states:

"In this particular instance we have a juror who's making financial decisions for the judge; that might very well be a valid basis for cause for a new trial. Maybe she would have felt pressured to convict because she didn't want to let the judge down. Maybe she would've been more biased toward his rulings because of that personal relationship where she's gonna lose money potentially if she loses him as a client. It could affect her pocketbook.

And so, this particular relationship is of importance. Had it merely been that she was his gardener, that would not have been a valid basis for cause. But when one's financial interest is at stake, I mean how many cases are there where people get in trouble for not disclosing their financial interest?"

Now I'm seeing red. *What's this guy insinuating?! That I would somehow profit or lose based on the outcome of this case?! How in the world would I know how the judge would rule in this case?!*

The judge speaks up, addressing the defense attorney:

"But if you never asked that question, are you saying that you have a duty as a juror to come forward when you've never been asked that question?"

He replies:

"Well, I believe she was asked that question because I know what questions I asked, Your Honor."

At this point, I feel totally slandered. My integrity and character have been called into question. I know beyond a shadow of a doubt that he never asked that question about knowing the judge.

The judge comments:

"I've gone through many trials where no one asked that question."

The defense attorney responds:

"And, Your Honor, the case law says very clearly that question must be asked. It says that the juror must have failed to answer or deliberately concealed the question, so if the question is not asked, you're right, then my point would be moot. You're absolutely right. But I contend it was."

I vigorously shake my head from where I'm sitting. I can't believe what I'm listening to.

The State jumps in:

"Your Honor, a judge is supposed to not be a party. They don't go for the defendant, against the defendant, for the State, against the State. They're a referee for all intents and purposes. So how is that prejudicial? They're not a party. They don't have an interest in the case. The jury doesn't have to please the judge, because as a judge you shouldn't be saying which way you're leaning."

The defense attorney continues to argue frantically that a mistrial *must* be found in this case. The judge eventually shuts things down and announces a recess will be held.

At this point, I'm nauseous and feel like I'm not getting enough air. I keep rubbing my "Be Still" tattoo as if it's brail that I'm reading. It hasn't healed all the way and is still slightly raised. I glance over toward the defendant and our eyes meet. She clasps her hands together and peers directly into my eyes with compassion. The floodgate of tears opens, and I look away. The recess seems to be taking forever. I rock back and forth in my seat and realize my medication for anxiety is having zero effect on me.

The judge enters the courtroom and begins to speak, but by this point, I'm not comprehending much. To my ear, she sounds like one of the adults in a Charlie Brown cartoon. Then I catch this sentence:

> "A mistrial is declared by this Court because of juror misconduct. This makes me sick, believe me. It just makes me sick that a four-day jury trial was had, jurors were inconvenienced for four days, they did their civic duty, and we must do it all again."

I'm stunned. I can't speak. A mistrial has been placed on *my* shoulders. Surely, this didn't *have* to be a mistrial. The judge continues to talk and give instructions, but I can't process any of it. Then she addresses me:

> "Ms. Robertson, the Court is serving on you an Order to Appear and Show Cause. It states, 'On this day comes now the Order to Appear and Show Cause, and after due consideration and other facts and matters before the Court, the Court doth find that Katrina Robertson shall appear on June 27th, 2022, at 10:00 o'clock, and

show cause why she should not be found in contempt of a Court order.'"

The bailiff brings me the paper and I numbly accept it. The State adds:

"The State would like to make a record that due to the fact a mistrial has been granted, we will be seeking charges of murder in the first-degree again, Your Honor."

I observe the defendant, and she's smiling broadly. *Does she not realize that things may be even worse for her now? Was there evidence or testimony that wasn't allowed in the first trial that will somehow be allowed in a second trial?* I feel bad for her. She has no idea how diligently I fought for her.

Eventually, court is adjourned, but I sit for a bit and try to let most people shuffle out ahead of me, especially Juror #8. Once I feel like my legs can carry me, I force myself to put one foot in front of the other and head toward the door, down the steps, and out the front door. To my right, I see Juror #8 speaking with two of the other jurors who I guess had decided to hang around till the hearing was over to see what happened. Juror #8 spots me and scurries off. I head toward the two others as tears begin to fall down my face. Juror #2 shouts, "Oh my God, Katrina! What happened? Are you all right?"

I point in the direction Juror #8 has gone and yell in a shaky voice, "She happened! She filed a complaint against me!"

"She's the nark?!" he exclaims. "You never even said anything! And the judge is granting a mistrial over that? Why?! Both of us testified that we didn't even hear any outside information brought in. What did she even complain about?"

"That I knew the judge and that I had looked the victim up in Court Connect and said I didn't find anything on him."

"Wow! What the crap, Katrina! That didn't even come into play with our deliberations or vote."

"Well, I've been found in contempt of court and have to go back on June 27th. I'm not okay. I'm probably going to have to get an attorney at this point."

"Man, I'm so sorry. Can you pull yourself up on Facebook on my phone here so we can stay in touch?"

"Yes, but I'm probably going to get off Facebook for a while after this. The defense attorney made a lot of harsh allegations against me, and I feel like I should disappear for a bit." We chat a little longer and then I tell them I need to just head home. He gives me an awkward hug, and I head to my car.

I get in my car and stare down at my tattoo. *I thought you were going to fight for me, God.*

I begin to head home, and a phone call comes through. A friend's name is displayed on the monitor in my car. I tap the screen to answer the call and try to choke out, "Hello?"

"Well friend, how did it go? Got it over with, right?"

I can't respond, and she realizes I'm too emotional to talk. I finally get out, "It's not good. I have to go back to court on June 27th."

"What? Why?!"

"I've been charged with contempt of court."

"Wow, Katrina! This is crazy!"

I arrive home and send a text to my husband, letting him know I have to go back to court. I can't handle another conversation right now. I begin to pull out things to try and put dinner together. *Do the normal things, Katrina; don't break down.* It's hard. There's a lump in my throat and my eyes keep blurring with tears. My son is sitting in the living room, and I need to keep it together for him.

The dogs start barking and there's a knock at the door. I'm not expecting anyone so I figure it must be a delivery or something. I peek out the window and see my friend standing there with a bouquet in her hands. I open the door; she offers me the flowers and then opens her arms for a hug. I fall into them, sobbing. We find our way back into the kitchen, where I had been preparing dinner, and begin preparing the flowers for a vase. I'm crying as I recount the court hearing to her. My son is still sitting in the living room and quietly slips out. He doesn't handle strong emotions well.

We take our conversation outside where the emotions come in waves out of me. This is a friend who has seen me in other low places. She listens; she cries with me. "What has happened!?" I almost yell at her. "How could that one statement I made cause this? The judge said I would be a *good* juror! Can you believe that? I bet he hates me now! The whole case must be redone!"

"Katrina, stop! You're going to make yourself sick! The judge probably feels horrible as well. Who would have ever thought this would happen?"

This is a friend who has her own present trials, and I ask her about those. She cries as she shares her current fears and the next steps in her journey. We cry as we share one another's burdens. "Friend, I love you," she whispers as we say our goodbyes.

Somehow, I manage to pull myself together to finish dinner, and I retire to my chair early. My husband is just angry at this point. He struggles to see me so beat down. I've been at low points, but this is my lowest. I want to go to sleep so everything disappears. I feel an ache in my body. I'm not sure if I'm allowed to communicate with the judge now or not, but I don't care; I *must* send him an apology. I pour my heart out in a text, knowing he probably can't and won't respond. I feel like I've at least gotten it off my chest.

An alarm goes off on my phone, and I raise it to look at the screen. A banner displays, "Check jury message." I stare at it. *Are you kidding me?!* Well, I know for certain I'm now excused from *all* jury duties forever and ever. I decide to humor the message and go check the jury messages. I log into my computer and navigate to the appropriate website. "January panel members. Your term has now expired." I can't help but chuckle. *Do you think you have jokes now, huh, God?*

> *"Though I walk in the midst of trouble, you preserve my life. You stretch out your hand against the anger of my foes; with your right hand you save me. The Lord will vindicate me; your love, Lord, endures forever—do not abandon the works of your hands." Psalm 138:7-8 NIV*

Thursday, May 12th, 2022

It's graduation day. I can't believe he's finally made it. This one we will be *dragging* across this stage. It's a big accomplishment for him. This is our biological son, and even though he hasn't suffered the kind of trauma our adopted sons have, things have still been a battle for him since the infant stages. He was diagnosed as being on the autism spectrum when he was five. I could write a book about the advocating I've had to do for him, but maybe, someday, he'll write a book about all he's overcome.

COVID is what nearly put the nails in the coffin of his education. It *did* put the nails in the education coffin for one of my adopted sons. School was already difficult for them to handle, and adding the turmoil of COVID on top of that load just made it heavier. When I think back on all the utter ridiculousness of the past two years, especially in the education system, I can feel the bile rise in the back of my throat. Forcing our kids to wear masks, people losing their jobs, businesses shutting down, bribing kids to get a vaccine, schools caring more about contact tracing than education, forcing kids to go to school "virtually," separating vaccinated from unvaccinated and applying different rules to people and students based on their vaccination status, requiring contact quarantines, canceling all social activities, etc.—I don't doubt that we'll continue to see for a couple of generations the collateral damage caused by our nation's reaction to this virus. Sure, some kids breezed straight through the whole ordeal and even thrived in a "virtual" environment. Many didn't, though. The kids in my home sure didn't, and the "at-risk" kids I work with fell through the cracks in record numbers. The fact that all this damage was done under the banner of "compassion" and "doing the right thing" leaves me reeling. Why can't people see the bigger picture?!

Then it hits me! Juror #8 may have reported me because she genuinely felt like she was doing the right thing. She may have felt like she was looking out for the "justice system." Sure, she didn't see eye to eye with me in the jury room, but she probably would have turned anyone in if she felt like they were "breaking rules." *Kind of like the "mask police,"* I think to myself and roll my eyes. Some people can't separate the Letter of the Law from the Spirit of the Law. And here we are, surveying the collateral damage. COVID is also one of the main reasons this trial was held so far after the crime.

The court system pretty much completely shut down for a year, and there certainly weren't any jury trials. Things got backlogged. But it was to keep people safe...right?

Anyway, it's graduation night, and it's being held *in person*. You can invite as many people as you want and sit where you want, and masks are optional. Finally, some common sense is reappearing. Despite his struggles, my son is graduating at the top of his class with high honors. Few know what a challenge this was for him. The graduation goes off without a hitch, the valedictorian gives an impressive speech, and we all cheer for our graduates as they toss their hats in the air.

Now the problematic part: try to connect with your graduate, in the crowd of thousands, while we all try to find our way to the single exit. We're like cattle, barely able to shuffle through the building. My exchange student is sticking close to me, but I lose my other son. He's no doubt catching up with old classmates. He'll be starting on his GED in a couple of months. I also lose my husband and in-laws. The exchange student and I find a place out of the way of the crowd, and I call my husband to see where he is. We yell through the phone our locations but then decide that we all just need to head to the front doors and meet there. We all spot one another, and we squeeze through the doors with the hundreds of others also trying to exit.

My in-laws have already made their escape from the crowd, but I holler at my husband that I want to get some pictures of our son in his cap and gown. We try to get a little further down the walkway, away from the crowd, to take some pictures. As we're walking, we spot a couple of individuals sprinting across the street to the parking lot, and then we see they're heading toward a fight that has broken out. We pause and watch for a minute. I get my boys' attention and tell them to ignore that so we can get a picture. I hand my phone to our exchange student so he can get a family shot of us. We squint nervously across the street as the fight has grown. Security has gotten involved, and people are swinging at the officers. It seems there are now several fights going on. People are still trying to exit the building and both the fight and the crowd watching it are growing larger by the second. My husband says, "Let's take pictures later before someone starts shooting," and begins to try and direct us further down the walkway, away from the commotion. Just as he does that, shots ring out, several of them. People begin to scream and hit the ground. One son dives for the bushes, another under a car, and another behind a car. I'm inspecting my surroundings, trying to assess what's happening, when my husband tackles me to the asphalt and yells at me, "Get down!"

A car squeals its tires and speeds off while the sirens start coming. We all begin a crouched scramble, ducking behind cars, trying to make it to our vehicles. We get in our cars and take the route *away* from the madness behind us. What in the world just happened?!

We get to the house and, trying to lighten the mood, I joke, "So can we take a picture now?" They laugh, but I continue, "Actually, I'm serious, I want a picture." My son picks up his hat and realizes he lost his tassel while diving for cover in a bush. "Well, you won't ever forget your graduation," I giggle. Then I turn toward our exchange student, "Welcome to America, kid." He's from Japan and guns are virtually nonexistent there. I'm not sure that I'll share this story with his family.

"The LORD is my rock, my fortress and my deliverer; my God is my rock, in whom I take refuge, my shield and the horn of my salvation. He is my stronghold, my refuge and my savior—from violent people you save me." 2 Samuel 22:2-3 NIV

Friday, May 13th, 2022

AFTER A TRAUMA-FILLED EVENING LAST night, I sleep in just a little and then try to get up to start as normal a day as possible. It doesn't last long. By 8:00 a.m., I am getting messages about the article in the paper. They had waited a day to write it, and now it's on the front page: "Mistrial Declared in Murder

Conviction." It shares the front page with the graduation shooting. I can only hope more people pay attention to that article rather than mine.

My mother-in-law sends the link to my husband, and he forwards it to me. I wonder why she didn't send it to me in our group chat. *She's probably embarrassed by me and thinks I'm an idiot,* I think to myself. I try to read the article but can't even finish it. It's awful. It even falsely reports that I looked up both the defendant and the victim. The beginning of it comments that I failed to disclose that I'm the financial advisor for the judge and that I work at a local wealth management company. I immediately go on Facebook and deactivate my account. The article goes on to quote the defense attorney as saying that this is "without a doubt a serious and grave issue not to be taken lightly" and—regarding myself—that "[she] might have felt pressure to vote the way the judge wanted since her financial interests were at stake." The room is spinning, and I'm sick to my stomach. I then get a message from my colleague and boss.

"Just wanted to be sure you know the newspaper released the story today about the trial. Praying for you. I know this is heavy on you. It will pass. Hang in there!"

"I'm so sorry. Not only do I not feel like I'll survive this, but I also don't even want to."

"Just remember to look at your arm. This sucks, but it'll be over, and God can somehow bring good out of even it."

"At least, the article doesn't mention our company directly. I've taken myself off Facebook."

"I'm not worried about the company, just you."

"Well, I'm not well."

"Trying to find words or actions to help. I can buy your lunch…"

"I can't even eat right now."

I'm so thankful for my work family. I don't deserve them. I shut the phone off and go lie down. There's no way I'm going to be able to get my brain to engage to do real work today. One of my boys has a doctor's appointment I need to get him to; I also have to get another son to a couple of tests he needs to take. At least I don't have to worry about cooking dinner. My in-laws are taking us out to dinner for my son's graduation.

One thing I do need to address today involves my volunteer role as a CASA, Court Appointed Special Advocate. I served as one for about four years, but then once we brought foster kids into our home, I had to resign. I was asked to come back and serve on the board a few years ago, and I did for a short time. I left before my term was up, though, because we were dealing with too much. I was asked again if I would come back, and I decided I would prefer to come back as a volunteer rather than a board member. I'm more of a hands-on person, and I enjoy building relationships with the kids and their families. I've always felt like the role of CASA gave me the most ability to help kids and families.

There's a different judge handling the dependent neglect cases now instead of the one from my previous time as a CASA, and I'm not impressed with this judge. There's also a whole lot more bureaucracy and political games being played now that I just don't want any part of. I had tried to resign a month or two ago but was talked out of it. I now know I must. Everything that doesn't have to be on my plate must go. I send an email to my supervisor and the director and tell them I just have too much going on right now and need to step away. My supervisor immediately calls me but I'm too emotional to answer. She calls again and then sends a text. I respond that I will call her when I'm able.

Once I've pulled myself together, I give her a callback. "What happened? What's going on?" she asks.

"It's nothing with either of my cases. I just have some stressful stuff going on right now and I need to step away. I know there are a lot of issues that need to be addressed right now with my cases and I don't mind being available to assist with things, provide information, etc., but I don't have time to keep up with time reports, write court reports, stuff like that."

"I understand," she answers. "Why don't I keep you assigned to these two cases, but I'll take over more. We really need to get that meeting done for the one case, but DHS isn't following through. Do you think you could send a Zoom link out to everyone with a meeting time?"

"Well, um…I've never set up a Zoom meeting before, but I'm sure I can figure it out. We do need to get a meeting done. I'll see what I can do."

We hang up, and I go to Zoom and realize it's easy to create a meeting and send the link for everyone to join. *Why the heck didn't DHS already do this,* I wonder. Frustrated, I set up a Zoom meeting for Monday and use my CASA email to send the link out to all the parties. I include my personal email address as well so that I'll get the link there to add the meeting to my calendar.

I've now gotten myself distracted enough that I'm able to do a few work items from my to-do list. Also, at the top of the list is finding an attorney. I give a call to one I've heard would be a good one to use. I leave a message with his assistant, and she asks for a few details of the case so she can run it by him and determine if it's even a case he can represent. "It's on the front page of the paper," I respond. She gives me a callback shortly and responds he can meet with me Monday. It's now already dinner time.

We meet my in-laws at the restaurant of my son's choosing. We settle at our table, and my son opens his gifts from his grandmother: a Bible she's read through and left notes for him in and a picture book she's put together of him from an infant to the present. I hope he knows what treasures these things are. I can't eat and mindlessly push my salad around on my plate. I'm doing good to just hold it together. Several times, I must swallow hard to keep the tears at bay. *What are they thinking of me?* I feel like the elephant in the room that no one wants to look at or speak to.

As we're leaving, my mother-in-law gives something to my husband, and then she takes my arm and places something in my hand. "And this is for you. A hug when you need it." The tears well up and I study what she's given me. It's a silver coin with a stick figure holding a heart balloon with a sun in the sky and the word "hug" on it. I wrap my arms around her and tell her thank you. I try to mumble something else, but the words won't come, so I awkwardly hang my head and try to get to the car before my emotions get the best of me.

I get in the car, take a deep breath, and wipe my tears away, trying to gather myself before my husband comes over. I've never been able to show too many emotions around him or he'll think it's something he's done and get angry, or he'll try to go fix whatever I'm upset about, and there just isn't any fixing this. When he gets in the car, I turn my head and stare out the window for the ride home.

> *"If your heart is broken, you'll find GOD*
> *right there; if you're kicked in the gut, he'll*
> *help you catch your breath." Psalm 34:18*
> *The Message*

Sunday, May 15th, 2022

ONE OF MY VERY BEST friends comes to visit with me for a bit after dinner. She has been going through her own hell, and we both point out the weight each of us has lost. "Stress sucks, doesn't it?!" I exclaim as we sit down on the patio couch.

"Yes, yes it does!" she replies.

We talk for an hour or two. I had invited her to watch a couple of videos with me that I thought might be helpful for her in her current storm, but she tells me she's just not ready to watch them. I get it. All my close friends have had tremendous battles in their lives. I'm so thankful that God handpicked girlfriends for me who "get the hard" and are here to sit with me in times of grief.

> *"Carry one another's burdens; in this way you will fulfill the law of Christ." Galatians 6:2 HCSB*

Monday, May 16th, 2022

THE APPOINTMENT WITH THE ATTORNEY I called on Friday is at 9:00 a.m. today. My husband and I arrive and wait nervously in the waiting area. I can't believe I'm having to do this. My mouth is going dry, and my nerves are getting the best of me. I've brought the statement that I had wanted to read in court. The door to the offices opens and he calls us back. We all take a seat in a conference room, and he puts a form in front of him that he's already jotted some notes on. It seems he's gotten himself a little familiar with the story, but I don't know what else to do but start from the beginning. He listens attentively. When I get to the part where I had asked to read my statement in court, I push my pages toward him. "I brought it with me today. Can I read it?"

"I'll be honest, Katrina. That's way too long for someone to listen to the whole thing. People will zone out after the first sentence or two."

"But I just wanted to apologize!" I cry, and then the tears come. "She wouldn't even let me speak! I could only answer with a 'yes' or 'no' to every question. Don't you think they would have listened when my emotions came with it?"

"That wasn't the right place for you to read that. This next hearing will be when you can apologize. I wouldn't suggest reading that or any prepared statement."

By now, the tears are falling freely. "What even is this next hearing? Is it where I state I'm guilty or not guilty?"

The attorney studies me and purses his lips together. "Katrina, you've already been found guilty. This is your sentencing hearing."

The room gets a little fuzzy and I catch my breath. "So...what does this mean for me?"

"Katrina, the maximum sentence for contempt of court is one year in jail."

I now have tunnel vision and I can no longer understand any of the words that are continuing to come out of his mouth. I'm certain I can't speak, either. My heart is pounding in my chest and my hands have gone clammy. I feel as if I've entered some sort of an alternate reality. *How is this happening?!* My mind screams as I try to ground myself.

The attorney studies the summons to "appear and show cause" that I had brought with me. "I've never seen anything like this before. I'm certain there's never been a case like this in our county. We've never had a juror come back and complain about another juror after a unanimous vote, and mistrials are beyond rare. They just don't happen. You're a unicorn, Katrina, and in new territory for me."

"But why should this have been a mistrial?" I choke out. "Is the judge that found the mistrial just trying to embarrass the original judge or make some sort of statement to the defense attorney? I feel like collateral damage in a messed-up system. I make one off-handed comment, that over half the jurors don't even remember, and she finds a mistrial?! Where's justice in all this?!"

"Our system is not built on justice as people like to believe. It's built on guilt or innocence."

I stare at him, perplexed, and I try to comprehend his statement. *What does he mean by no justice in our justice system?* "But the testimony of the jurors shows pretty clearly that I wasn't trying to persuade or prejudice anyone!"

"I feel bad for you, Katrina; I really do. You did something that we're all aware happens all the time. There's no doubt people look information up, talk to people, etc. You were just unfortunate enough to have someone complain about it. You're going to get through this."

The emotions flood me again when I hear that because there's a part of me that honestly doesn't believe I'm going to get through this. "But I don't even understand these rules for the jurors anyway. If we're the ones tasked with determining if another person is guilty or innocent, shouldn't we have access to all information? This isn't like it's 1930 and the only information we could access is maybe old newspapers and second-hand, biased info. We can literally pull up unbiased, factual information with just a few keystrokes. I'm not talking about social media. I'm talking about public records."

"I understand what you're saying, and maybe the rules are outdated, but they're still there."

My frustration builds. "Wouldn't a judge have access to that information in a case?"

"Sure, but it's highly unlikely that they would access it. They would only use the information presented in the trial."

"But they could, right? And the judge was able to know what all those witnesses were to testify, what the objections were, and why it wasn't allowed. But we, as the jurors, or the judge, in this case, can't know that information? We can't even ask questions of witnesses. How is that right?"

"You're not going to change the whole way we do things. The problem is jurors don't know the law and why certain things can't be admitted as evidence."

Now I'm angry. "Ah, so we're too stupid to figure out what's relevant and what's not?! Then maybe we need to do away with the entire jury system then!"

He allows me to simmer down, and I shed a few more tears. "I think I can help you, Katrina. I need you to know that I feel like a win will be ten days in jail. You don't need to decide right now." He writes $2,500 on the piece of paper in front of him and pushes it toward me. "That's my fee if you want me to represent you."

I still can't wrap my mind around doing jail time. I push my statement back toward him. "Will you read this?"

"I can't look at anything until we have a contract in place. You can contact my office if you have any questions and come by to sign papers if you decide you want to move forward."

We've been meeting for over an hour, and I'm completely exhausted. I gather my things and thank him for his time. I tell him I'll be in touch. I notice a couple of texts that have come through from individuals who were supposed to be part of the Zoom meeting this afternoon asking me what was going on. *Not sure what that's about.*

My mind is blank as I head home. Somehow, I must figure out how to keep functioning. Shutting down just isn't an option. Plus, I must pull myself together for that Zoom meeting for one of my CASA kids. This kid has been the victim of one injustice after another, and no one has been willing to put up a good fight for him. I'm angry. I worked my tail off to get him into a program to earn his diploma and get certified in welding, which he loves, and he's gotten kicked out. Now we all need to put our heads together to figure out where he goes next. He's one of the many I've fought for only to have it all fall apart.

I sit down at my computer and open up my personal email to see a reply from my CASA supervisor regarding the Zoom meeting link I'd sent out. It looks like she's used the "reply all" function to contact everyone in my original email group, but she's left out my CASA email address. She's telling everyone the meeting is canceled due to my resignation. This is what those texts were about! Those people were supposed to be part of the meeting as well. I'm so angry I could spit fire! She was going to let me start that Zoom meeting and be the only one to show up! She probably didn't realize my personal email was a part of the group. I'm pretty sure what happened is that the director told the supervisor to cancel the meeting because I had emailed the two of them that I needed to resign. The director probably doesn't realize that the supervisor had asked me to continue to help, specifically with that meeting. I quickly type out an email to the supervisor. "Hmmm, thought you said you were keeping me on those cases. Are you not able to still lead the Zoom? Seems silly to completely cancel it as it needs to be done. As for me, I'll gladly bow out."

She responds, with the director included, that she didn't ask me to set up the Zoom. I'm so confused. *Why is she acting this way toward me?* I've always gotten along with her. I tell her I just really feel beat down at the moment. To which she responds:

> "My response to your email was clear. I am not about to go back and forth regarding something so simple. At no time did I ever say or do anything to beat you down. I have backed you up on a lot of things, but I will not go back and forth on something I didn't do. I have to work all my cases, and this is where my time will be spent."

I'm seething now. *Why do I continually get sucker punched for simply trying to help?!* I type out another reply, "Wow...I only said I *feel* beat down. I didn't say you did it. I just thought it would have been nice if you'd contacted me directly and said, 'We will handle it from here since you requested to resign. I know I said I would keep you on these two cases, but you seem overwhelmed. Thanks for the help you were able to give.' I get your message now though. I'll be adjusting our family trust and removing CASA from it." I then take the trust document from a file, draw a line through the part listing CASA as a beneficiary, take a picture, and send it to her. Necessary? Probably not.

I send her a private message. "You're an amazing person. You work hard, you fight hard, and you love hard. I thought of you as a friend and a fellow 'fighter.' There are many reasons for my decision to resign, that I won't go into, but at the end of it, I'm just under insurmountable stress. I felt punched in the gut when I was contacted by other people on the email chain about the Zoom being canceled, instead of you directly. I know CASA is a good organization with good intentions; they've been part of my heart for years. I can no longer support it, though."

I never get a response. Bridge burned. Not the finest moment in my anger, but it was time to move on from CASA anyway.

I examine my calendar and realize I have a lady I'm supposed to get to a doctor's appointment. It's probably a good thing, as, otherwise, I would just curl into the fetal position for the rest of the day. This lady is needy and a handful. She has no one, except me. What started with a friend asking if I could help pick up groceries for a lady whom she'd seen struggling at a bus stop, had turned into me becoming this lady's POA, handling all her doctor appointments, paying all her bills, getting her moved twice into assisted living facilities, and overall being the only person in her life to call when she has a need. *Who does that?! Me...apparently, I do that.*

My husband helps people all day, every day in his role as a chaplain. He just swoops in with encouraging words, but then he steps out. There's more to it than that, but he can help people without getting as emotionally involved as I tend to do. I'm hoping my days with the constant barrage of needy people will become less now that I've removed CASA from my life. I'm thankful for the people it has enabled me to help but it's time to move on. I'm ready for a less involved role, like maybe sending someone a card! No more taking custody of kids, getting guardianship, adopting, getting power of attorney for people, making endless phone calls, sending countless emails, etc. I'm tired. *Just breathe in, breathe out.*

> *"So we must not get tired of doing good, for*
> *we will reap at the proper time if we don't*
> *give up." Galatians 6:9 HCSB*

Tuesday, May 17th, 2022

It's my mom's birthday and, although I've shared all my current drama with my brothers, I've kept it from my mom. It would stress her out and she would worry about me. She rents a house from us that's right behind us. One of my brothers rents our little cottage that we had originally built for our disabled son and which sits directly next to our house. I like having family close. They come over often for dinner. Today, my husband and I are looking for a house to buy that our daughter and her husband could rent from us. We view one that we decide to put an offer on. It's a lowball offer, but the real estate agent is with us in agreeing that they're asking too much. Houses are selling for crazy amounts right now. The agent is a friend whom we have worked with several times over the years. I share my current court debacle with her, and she's flabbergasted. "I'll be at that hearing on June 27th, Katrina!" I'm surprised she would take time out of her day for me like that.

"I'm leaving from here to go retain an attorney," I tell her. I arrive at the attorney's office, hand them a check, and sign the papers. I can't believe jury duty has led to this.

Me with my mom and three brothers.

"For our battle is not against flesh and blood, but against the rulers, against the authorities, against the world powers of this darkness, against the spiritual forces of evil in the heavens." Ephesians 6:12 HCSB

Thursday, May 19th, 2022

I WALK INTO MY SON'S room in the morning to give him his meds and get him up for the day. Should I be doing this for a nearly eighteen-year-old? No. He's much more pleasant once he's had his meds, though, so I just prefer to wake him with them. He moans as he tries to sit up and rubs his neck. "My throat hurts so bad. Well, it's like my neck—I can't even really turn my head."

He winces as he swallows his pills and seems to almost choke on them. I feel around his neck, and it does seem like there's some swelling. Maybe his lymph nodes? I decide to send the doctor a quick message to see if he can see him. The nurse responds that the doctor can see him that afternoon. *Wow, that doesn't happen often.*

I bring him to the office, and he holds his head in a very stiff position, not looking up, down, or to the side. The doctor examines his throat and then feels around his neck. His fingers hit a spot close to the center of his neck and my son winces and jumps a little. "Right there where this knot is, huh?" the doctor asks.

"Yeah," my son replies. "It's painful to move my head side to side but hurts really bad to look up. Difficult to swallow too."

"That's not where a lymph node would be, is it?" I ask the doctor.

"No, that's where the thyroid is. I'm concerned he's got a nodule on it. I'm going to send him over for an ultrasound. It may be next week before they can get him in. I'll call personally and see if they can work him in as soon as possible."

I've used this doctor for years. He's walked through a *lot* of challenges with my "trauma" kids and has always been a big advocate for getting them the help they need. We leave the office, and the hospital calls by the time I get home to let me know they can get my son in for an ultrasound at noon the next day. I'm thankful they can get him in so quickly, as my son seems to be in legitimate discomfort.

> *"I have told you these things so that in Me you may have peace. You will have suffering in this world. Be courageous! I have conquered the world." John 16:33 HCSB*

Friday, May 20th, 2022

I START THE DAY EARLY with some conference calls for work. Work has been a little more stressful than normal lately as the markets have pretty much done nothing but tank since January. It's never fun reporting to clients that they have losses. I feel a huge responsibility toward my clients. They depend on me to be watching out for them and helping them forge the best financial plans they can. When the markets are as volatile as they are right now, it gets increasingly difficult because some of them want to make emotionally-based decisions that often lead to financial suicide. I try to hold their hand through the storms, but at the end of the day, they're the captain, and I'm only the navigator. I can tell them how to get somewhere, but if they tell me to do something else, I have no choice but to follow their instructions.

Noon finally arrives, and I load my son up to take him to the hospital for the ultrasound. They take him back to the ultrasound room and my husband joins us; he works as a chaplain at the hospital. I can tell the tech has "found something" but, of course, doesn't mention what. She continues to move the wand around on his neck while clicking the mouse for the computer, changing the view, and taking measurements. She finishes up, wipes the gel from his neck, and tells us the doctor will see it and send a report to his primary doctor.

We take our time leaving the hospital, chatting with my husband. By the time we're heading home, my son's doctor's office is already calling. "Your son does have a nodule on his thyroid, and the doctor wants to get him into an endocrinologist at the children's hospital as soon as possible. Appointments are usually months out in scheduling but he's going to speak to the doctor himself to see if he can get him in quickly," the nurse tells me.

I must remind myself to breathe. For the doctor to call that quickly can't be a good sign. I know the report should already be available in my son's medical portal, so I decide I'm going to open it as soon as I get home. I call my husband and give him the update. He asks me to send the report to him when I get it. He has doctor friends at the hospital; I'm sure he wants to get opinions from them.

I pull the report up on my computer. I have to Google nearly every other word to make sense of it. At the bottom, under the summary, a sentence reads, "Highly suspicious of malignancy. Biopsy needed." I just stare at it, blinking. *Cancer?! Is that what I must deal with now?!*

> *"I cry out loudly to* GOD, *loudly I plead with* GOD *for mercy. I spill out all my complaints before him, and spell out my troubles in detail." Psalm 142:1-2 The Message*

Monday, May 23rd, 2022

I'M SENDING MESSAGES TO THE mom of the girl I call my "bonus daughter." This girl lived with us for a period when her mom had serious spinal reconstruction surgery. She's gone on many of our family vacations with us and is generally just part of the family at this point. She went through the same thing with her thyroid, and we were nearly certain it was thyroid cancer. It ended up not being malignant, but she was diagnosed with Hashimoto's, a thyroid disease. It's bizarre to be going through this with another kid. I send some of my son's lab results and the ultrasound report to the mom since she's familiar with thyroid issues. I tell her that the endocrinologist has already called with an appointment for him on Friday.

"Wow! I've never heard of getting in that quick! Remember how it took months for us to get in?!"

"I know," I reply. "I'm not sure if it causes me to be even more nervous that they're rushing it like this. I'm sure his doctor is pulling strings for us."

Me with my "bonus" daughter.

My day is filled with more work appointments, and I push all the other stresses in my life away so I can give my clients my full attention. One meeting is with clients whom I'm helping to retire early. It's a good meeting, and they leave happy. That invokes happiness in me. I love being able to help people reach their retirement goals.

After dinner, I retire to my chair with my book and my dogs. One son is at work and my husband is mountain biking with another. The exchange student comes downstairs and joins me in the living room. I put my book aside so I can chat with him. He only has a couple of weeks left with us. He actually has three weeks left in the United States, but his family is coming from Japan, and they're going to spend a week or so on the East Coast. He comes to my office often, or the living room when I'm reading, to chat, and I enjoy our conversations. I ask him if he's sad to be leaving or excited to be going home.

"I will miss it here. I wish I could stay for two years," he confides.

I can tell that putting a finger on his different emotions and translating it to English appropriately is a challenge for him. He's had one heck of a year, and I hope I've been able to give him the experience he wanted. "Has this been what you expected? Have you learned what you wanted to?"

He pauses for a long time, petting a dog in his lap. "I didn't know what to expect, but it has been a very good experience. The most amazing thing I've experienced is you."

I cock my head to one side, not sure what he's trying to communicate, and wait for him to continue.

"The way you love people. It truly is amazing." His eyes fill up with tears. "I've watched how you care for people for the whole year, and it leaves me amazed."

I'm not sure how to respond to him. I feel like this is a compliment, but I don't take compliments well. "I just do what I feel like I'm supposed to do, I guess."

"Thank you for taking care of me like your own son. I love you like you're my mother."

I smile at him. "And you have been a joy to have in our home, and I look forward to watching where life takes you. You're not allowed to lose contact with us!"

We chat a while longer and he tells me goodnight and heads back upstairs to his room. I breathe in deeply. That's what it's all about, right—love? Even if it doesn't always produce what you want it to.

Me with our exchange student.

"If I speak with human eloquence and angelic ecstasy but don't love, I'm nothing but the creaking of a rusty gate." 1 Corinthians 13:1 The Message

I'VE STAYED IN TOUCH WITH the school counselor who was involved in one of my CASA cases so we can continue to discuss one of the kids we were both advocating for. This case needs someone who will shake the bushes and get people to do their jobs. I'm no longer that person, and I feel bad for the kid. The counselor was one of the ones who had messaged me confused when the email came through that the meeting had been canceled because I'd resigned. I don't share all the details behind my resignation and just mention I've been under a lot of stress.

"Just know that I think you're amazing! Truly!" she sends me in a text. "Are you available to get together this evening for some drinks and cheese dip? You can share some of what's going on if you want."

Cheese dip and drinks! She's now speaking my love language! "I don't know if you want me unloading all my ridiculous crap!"

"I'm here for it!" she quickly responds.

We decide to meet up. She's a school counselor but an "all-in" one and cut from the same cloth I am. I was once able to talk her into moving a kid in with her, so there's that. I speak at ease with her and share the court proceedings and then the current thyroid scare we're having with my boy. I get emotional with her when I talk about all the CASA kids and families I feel like I helped in vain. "I just want to know that it's all worth it. You know?"

She listens to all of it attentively. "I want to come to your court date if I can."

"If I give everything I own to the poor and
even go to the stake to be burned as a martyr,

but I don't love, I've gotten nowhere. So,
no matter what I say, what I believe, and
what I do, I'm bankrupt without love." 1
Corinthians 13:3 The Message

Thursday, May 26th, 2022

I'M ON THE ROAD BY 6:30 a.m. I have to get one of my prior
CASA kids and his mom to an 8:00 a.m. appointment
with his endocrinologist who's an hour away. He's a severe
diabetic, and they have no vehicle. I arrive at their apartment
at 6:45 a.m., and they're waiting outside for me. This mom
and her boy have been through so much. She hasn't been
the perfect parent, by any means, but she's not had anything
come to her easily, either. She hobbles over to my car with her
cane and gets in. She's younger than me but appears much
older. "Thank you so much! You have no idea how much I
appreciate you!" she exclaims as she shuts the door.

"No problem, glad I can help," I reply as I confirm
her son has fastened his seatbelt behind me. She has packed
some food for them both to eat on the way, but she's sure he
checks his blood sugar first so she knows how much insulin
to dose him with. She proudly shows me all his blood sugar
recordings she has kept up with and the folder she has of all
the important paperwork they may need for the appointment.

We're well into our hour-long trip to Little Rock when
several emergency vehicles pass us, going the other direction.
No doubt there's been a wreck. This highway is awful right
now with the never-ending construction. Five minutes later
my phone rings and I see it's my daughter calling. She would
be on this same highway right now, going the other direction,
on the way to work.

"Hello?" I answer.

There's nothing but sobbing on the line.

"Are you okay?!" My heart is now beating in my throat. *Has she been in a wreck? Were all those emergency vehicles for her?*

There's a deep breath on the line as she tries to catch her breath. "Mom? I just saw the worst wreck ever! A lady was pulling a child out of a car, he was bleeding and didn't look like he was responding!"

"Are you still driving?"

"Yes," she manages to get out between sobs.

"I need you to find a safe place to pull over right now."

"Okay, I'm pulling into that old gas station now."

I tell her to take some deep breaths and stay put until she's calmed down. We talk a while longer until she seems better. I call my husband and tell him to check on her in a bit. We've got to find a place in town for her and her husband so she's not having to do this commute anymore.

We arrive at the clinic on time, and I let the mom handle everything. She listens to the doctor, takes notes, asks questions, talks about concerns, etc. I'm proud of her; she's trying. I worry, though; she has a lot to overcome. What if her son ends up back in foster care after his mom and I have worked so earnestly to get him home?

On the drive back home, a call comes through that I take. I talk about the hearing coming up on June 27th.

"You have to go to court?" the mom asks when I get off the phone. "Is everything okay?"

"Not really." I'm not sure how much to share with her. "Remember when I told you I couldn't help that one day because I had jury duty? Well, another jury member ended up complaining about me, and now I've been charged with contempt of court and have to go back to court."

"Oh my gosh, Katrina! Why would they do that to you? You've been like an angel; a true God send. No one has ever stepped in to help me as you did. I wouldn't have my son back if it weren't for you. Can I come to court with you? There's no way I can ever repay you for what you've done for us."

I fight back the tears and pat her hand. "You just take care of that boy. That's how you can thank me."

We arrive back at their apartment, and her son gets out to help his mom. He turns around and sticks his head back in the door. "Miss Katrina, thank you. Thank you for everything."

I head back to the house and announce my arrival to the two boys at home. I've made arrangements for us to go horseback riding this afternoon. It's something our exchange student has never done and probably won't ever have an opportunity to do again.

"You guys ready?" I holler up the stairs. They come down, and I confirm they're both wearing closed-toe shoes. It's a pretty day but a little chilly. We make it to the horse stables where we are given instructions and pointed to our horses. I sit back on my horse and watch the exchange student nervously climb up on his horse. I love watching people experience new things. We amble our way through the woods, and I breathe in the fresh, crisp air. *You're going to be okay, Katrina. Breathe in, breathe out.*

"He executes justice for the fatherless and the widow, and loves the foreigner, giving him food and clothing." Deuteronomy 10:18 HCSB

Friday, May 27th, 2022

JUST A LITTLE OVER TWENTY-FOUR hours later, I'm back at the same endocrine office with a different kid, this time my own. Ironically, I'll be bringing my "bonus daughter" here next week, as well. They all are seeing different doctors in the clinic for different issues. The doctor who's seeing my son for his thyroid nodule has already reviewed both the report and the ultrasound when we arrive. He asks a lot of questions, some involving family history, which is a little tricky since this son is adopted.

Fortunately, I do have a relationship with his biological parents. This son has a deep bond with his biological family, and I knew when he came to live with us that he would, either on purpose or accidentally, eventually find them. They don't even live far from us. I got ahead of him on it and reached out to them to get to know them before I started allowing visits. It's not a conventional setup, but it works. They respect me as his parent, and it's been good for him to still have contact with them. They aren't "bad" people. They had a rough start in life, going in and out of foster care themselves as children. His mom became pregnant with her first child at just fourteen years old. At some point, they crossed from being victims of trauma, abuse, and neglect to being the perpetrators of it. I see it all the time; it's a generational thing that's nearly impossible to destroy.

I had reached out to his bio mom before the appointment to see if she knew if there were any thyroid issues in the family. She'd said she wasn't aware of any and even called some aunts and cousins.

Blessed with the involvement of both bio and adoptive family.

The doctor continues to ask questions and seems genuinely concerned about what may be going on. He says a biopsy needs to be done. Fortunately, it's no longer causing my son any more discomfort, and the doctor thinks this is due to the bleeding out of some of the fluid that was in it. Because it's not causing discomfort, he sends a referral for a needle biopsy, which will be less invasive.

On the hour-long drive home, I get a call that his biopsy is scheduled for June 7th. I'm glad we'll get it done before the court date.

> *"He predestined us to be adopted through Jesus Christ for Himself, according to His favor and will." Ephesians 1:5 HCSB*

Sunday, May 29th, 2022

A GIRL I'VE BEEN FRIENDS with since literally grade school is in town. She currently lives a little over three hours away, but her mom is still here in town. We met in third grade when we were classmates, and then in fifth grade, we lived down the street from each other. I changed schools in the sixth grade, but we continued to be friends through high school. She was a bridesmaid at my wedding, but our lives went in different directions after that. We stay in touch via Facebook, and once every few years we find a way to get together. It's been years since we've last gotten together, but recently I had reached out to her one evening through text to tell her I was in a bit of a nightmare. She tells me she wants to come over and hear more about what's been going on.

We sit on the porch and chat, getting caught up on one another's lives. I dive into the jury duty story, finishing without getting emotional.

"That's all so bizarre, Katrina. I want to be here for you in court next month," she says sincerely.

"There's no reason for you to take off work and drive all the way here for that."

"No, I want to."

I'm taken aback by the gesture. *We haven't maintained a relationship over the years, yet she's willing to sacrifice an entire day for me?* There are family members on my husband's side who are not even responding to my texts asking if they will come to court; even worse, one replied that she won't support me. Talk about feeling like you have to pull a knife out of your back. That hurts.

"Thank you," I manage to get out. "Means a lot to me."

Circa 1986. Third grade with my longest-standing friend and yes, I'm still that much taller than her.

"Open your mouth for the people who cannot speak, for the rights of all the unfortunate." Proverbs 31:8 NASB

Wednesday, June 1st, 2022

I RECEIVE AN EMAIL WITH a transcript of the May 11th hearing, along with a bill for $397.70. *Awfully expensive digital file!* My attorney had requested this, along with the transcript from voir dire. I immediately print it out and read every bit of it. My anger, frustration, and anxiety overwhelm me all over again as I relive the hearing. The defense attorney has me seething. I feel like I could file a defamation suit against him. I sit down to type out an email to my attorney.

The defense attorney says I lied, I failed to disclose my relationship with the judge, and then even went so far as an accusation that "my financial interests were at stake." I've looked up the five things that must be proved for defamation and they are:

- A statement of fact. Of course, for defamation to have occurred, somebody must have made a statement that's considered defamatory. **He stated all three above as facts.**
- A published statement. **This was said both in court and then published in newspapers on the front page.**
- The statement caused injury. **I have been sick, and my mental and emotional health is a wreck. I also felt the need to take myself off social media which is where I do a lot of my business advertising. It has caused injury to my reputation, and I've already experienced a direct effect on my personal relationships. It can affect my professional reputation as well, especially since I am the CCO of my firm. His false accusations call into question the integrity of me in my position to those who have placed their trust in me to fulfill the responsibilities of my position. It can also harm not only me but because I'm an officer of the firm, also cause harm to the entire firm. It also cost me all the legal fees and fees to get transcripts printed to prove that he was lying.**
- The statement must be false. **All the statements are 100% false.**
- The statement is not privileged. **Me being *anyone's* financial advisor is completely confidential.**

I hit "send" and try to find something to do to take my mind off it. With what I've found out about that defense attorney, I don't believe he should even be practicing law. *Is he just trying to keep his hands in his client's pockets by asking for a mistrial?*

My attorney responds and tells me he just doesn't see a defamation case. My "losses" would be hard to calculate, and that's the most important part of defamation. He tells me I'm welcome to get a second opinion. I'm not interested in that. The reality is, I'm not that interested in a defamation case. I'm just angry, and I want all this nonsense over.

> *"Have mercy on me, my God, have mercy on me, for in you I take refuge. I will take refuge in the shadow of your wings until the disaster has passed. I cry out to God Most High, to God, who vindicates me." Psalm 57:1-2 NIV*

Friday, June 3rd, 2022

I HAD TOLD MY ATTORNEY that I could get character reference letters for him if that would be helpful. He tells me that letters can't be admitted as evidence, but he doesn't mind reading them and seeing if there's anyone he may want to call as a witness on my behalf. I've had lots of people ask me how they can help, so I tell them they're welcome to write a letter if they wish. I've gotten ten or so back, and I've forwarded them to my attorney. Their kind words about me are overwhelming.

I also knew the judge who would be hearing my case is Catholic, and I was pretty sure I knew who her priest was. I thought he would be a very credible witness for me, so my husband reached out to him and asked if we could meet.

Today is the day of our visit. I feel desperate pouring my story out to this priest. He listens attentively and patiently while taking notes. I feel like I'm in confession, and the tears flow freely. As I begin to run out of things to tell him, he says, "Katrina, I want to help any way I can. I'll write a letter for you, but I'll also be at the hearing. If nothing else, my collar sometimes brings some calm to places."

I wipe my tears and thank him for his time and head to my car. I continue to try and gather myself together before driving home. I have to take our exchange student to Little Rock tonight. We're spending the night there because he has to be at the airport at 5:00 a.m. to catch a flight to New York to meet his family. *Breathe in, breathe out.* Somehow, I think I've managed to keep most of my crazy from him.

> *"I consider that our present sufferings are not worth comparing with the glory that will be revealed in us." Romans 8:18 NIV*

Saturday, June 4th, 2022

I'M BACK HOME FROM THE airport by 6:00 a.m. and lie down to rest for a bit. I have several things planned for this Saturday. It's the birthday of the lady whom I help often, so I tell her I'll pick her up and take her to lunch at her favorite buffet. We're waiting to be seated when I hear, "Hey, Katrina!" and someone hugs me from behind. I turn to see the face of a "kid" who lived with us many years ago. He was one of my CASA kids at one time but then ended up living with us while I helped him get his GED. His father had gone to prison and his mom had bad addiction issues. The judge gave us guardianship to keep him from going back to foster care.

Fortunately, he did obtain his GED, but unfortunately, he moved back in with his dad when his dad got out of prison. His father had health issues, and he felt like he should help take care of his dad. No amount of pleading would get him to stay with us and continue with his education. I saw the writing on the wall when he moved out. It wasn't long before the cycle of being in and out of jail started. He got married, divorced, lost custody of a kid, etc. Same story, different kid. Breaks my heart every time. He appears to be doing decently right now and is trying. I've heard he has another baby on the way.

"You won't believe the mess I'm in right now," I start. "Served on a jury, was complained about, got charged with contempt of court, and now I have a court date and the possibility of jail time."

"No way, Katrina!" he exclaims. "There's no way a judge can put you in jail. You help too many people!" He glances at the lady I'm with and seems to know she's someone I've taken under my wing. "When's your court date? I'll try to be there if I can get off work."

"June 27th," I tell him. "You still have the same number?"

"Yes, ma'am."

"I'll send you a text tonight and explain more. Are you staying out of trouble?"

"Yes, ma'am. Just working. I'm not getting enough hours."

"I'm assuming you're still painting?"

"Yes, ma'am."

"I know a guy looking for a painter. I'll get you in touch with him tonight."

"That would be awesome! Thank you so much! It sure is good seeing you."

"Good seeing you too. Keep your head on straight!"

When he was living with us and about to be baptized.

"Defend the weak and the fatherless; uphold the cause of the poor and the oppressed. Rescue the weak and the needy; deliver them from the hand of the wicked." Psalm 82:3-4 NIV

Monday, June 6th, 2022

I'M TEXTING A FRIEND AND I tell her I have no idea what I'm supposed to wear to court on the 27th.

"Wear purple. It's your favorite color and suits you. Purple is the color of royalty; put it on and claim it! You're a child of the King! Here's your dress." She sends me a link to a purple dress on Amazon. "Oh, and I'll wear purple to court to support you too," she adds.

As tears roll down my face, I hit, "Add to cart." I don't deserve friends this good.

At an event where we ironically were both wearing purple.

*"She is clothed with strength and dignity;
she can laugh at the days to come." Proverbs
31:25 NIV*

Tuesday, June 7th, 2022

It's the day of my son's biopsy. He doesn't have to be there till noon and can't eat before, so I let him sleep in. As for me, I wake with my normal nausea. Every. Single. Morning.

The pit in my stomach stays around most of the day, but for some reason, mornings are the worst. Trying to get my teeth brushed without triggering the gag reflex is almost impossible. I'm also dealing with daily headaches and near panic attacks that hit me at random times throughout the day. I feel like I'm losing my mind, and I've lost too much weight. I decide to send a message to my doctor to see if he can get me some meds to help. We have a long-term, good relationship. I send the message to his nurse. I explain some of the stress in my life and the symptoms it's causing. She gets back to me quickly that the doctor is sending over stuff for nausea, headaches, and anxiety. I thank her and tell her it will hopefully be over on the 27th.

An email then comes through from my attorney letting me know that he has requested a continuance on my case. *Wait?! What?! I don't want this continued; I want it over!* His reasons make sense though. We still have not received all of the transcripts we requested. Another reason for getting a continuance—one that we didn't officially share with the court—is that the retrial for the defendant hasn't taken place. My attorney is hoping the retrial will happen before my hearing. If the defendant ends up with a harsher sentence, it's going to look bad for the defense attorney.

I'm glad my doctor is sending me meds; I need them. I decide to also send my therapist a message and tell her I need to get back in to see her again. I saw her when things got bad with my disabled son, but after that, I had thought my life was getting to a better place of "normal" and quit going.

It's almost time to head to the surgery appointment, but I send one more email to my attorney. "Is it possible to ask for a different judge for the hearing? She decided my actions were bad enough to cause a mistrial, so I don't see how she would do anything but give me a harsh sentence."

He responds that the judge is not going to recuse herself from a contempt of court charge, especially when it happened in another courtroom. There are no grounds to ask for a different judge. *Of course*, I think...

It's time to head to the children's hospital with my son. I load him up, and we start the hour-long drive. He doesn't seem too nervous, but he peppers all the nurses and doctors with dozens of questions when we arrive. I'm able to stay with him in pre-op until they're ready to take him back. He spends his time flirting with nurses and enjoying getting smiles out of them. This one makes me crazy but can pack on the charm. They roll him back to the operating room, and I retire to the waiting area.

The procedure doesn't take long, and the doctor comes to the waiting room to give me an update. He lets me know they were able to get good samples and are sending them to pathology. I should hear back in a couple of days. He leads me back to post-op where my son is slowly waking up.

He's grumpy and confused but begins to come around. They get him a drink and tell him that, once he feels steady enough to get dressed, we're free to go. He tries to stand and wobbles a little but refuses assistance. He manages to get himself dressed, and a nurse says I can pull my car around to the front, and she will wheel him down. "I don't need a wheelchair!" he declares.

"Sorry, it's the rule. You must leave in a wheelchair," the nurse explains.

"Fine, but I'm rolling it myself," he insists.

"Stubborn, that one is," I say with exasperation to the nurse as I leave him with her and head to the car.

I reach the house in time to start dinner, and I begin sending messages to people to let them know that my attorney has asked for a continuance on the case. I then send a message to my tattoo artist with a picture of the word "breathe" in a fancy script. "I need this on my other forearm," I text to him.

"I can get you in tomorrow," he responds.

This is unprecedented for him. He stays booked out for months.

"See you then," I respond, and then retire to my chair to read. *Breathe in, breathe out.*

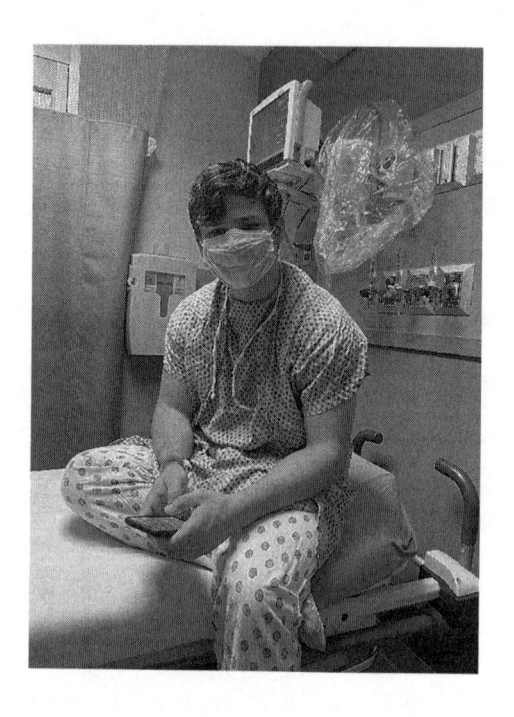

"You are my hiding place; you will protect me from trouble and surround me with songs of deliverance." Psalm 32:7 NIV

Wednesday, June 8th, 2022

My appointment for the tattoo is at 9:00 a.m. *Who gets tattoos that early?!* Me, apparently. I settle into the chair. "So, you know how I told you I had just finished jury duty the last time I was here?"

"Yeah."

"Well, you're not going to believe what all that turned into." I go into the story while he works on my arm. Like everyone who hears the story, he mainly just shakes his head, uttering things like, "I just can't believe that."

He finishes up and I admire the finished product. I have a *full* day ahead of me, including a funeral for one of my husband's uncles. *Breathe in, breathe out.*

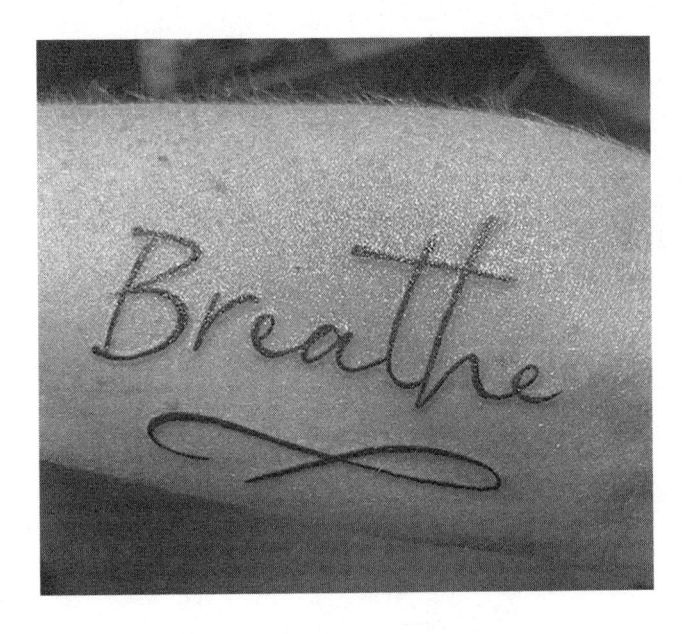

"Let everything that breathes praise the Lord. Hallelujah!" Psalm 150:6 HCSB

Friday, June 10th, 2022

I RECEIVE A NOTIFICATION THAT my son has a report on his medical portal. I expect it to be the biopsy results, so I quickly click the link to get to it. I pause for a minute before opening the document and take a deep breath. I open it and scan it. "Normal benign thyroid growth. No malignancy found." *Praise Jesus! Finally, some good news!*

As for me, one of my eyes has gotten red and irritated. I try leaving my contacts out but it's not getting better. I wonder if it's pink eye. I don't think it's worth a doctor's appointment; I just need some antibiotic drops to see if that clears it up. I decide to send a picture to a friend who is an APN. She's not convinced it's pink eye, but she does send me a prescription for eye drops. I pick them up, start using them, and decide I'll stay out of my contacts for a while.

> *"Why would you ever complain, O Jacob, or, whine, Israel, saying, 'GOD has lost track of me. He doesn't care what happens to me'? Don't you know anything? Haven't you been listening? GOD doesn't come and go. God lasts. He's Creator of all you can see or imagine. He doesn't get tired out, doesn't pause to catch his breath. And he knows everything, inside and out. He energizes those who get tired, gives fresh strength to dropouts. For even young people tire and drop out, young folk in their prime stumble and fall. But those who wait upon GOD get fresh strength. They spread their wings and soar like eagles, they run and don't get tired, they walk and don't lag behind." Isaiah 40:27-31 The Message*

Saturday, June 11ᵗʰ, 2022

OUR EXCHANGE STUDENT IS RETURNING late tonight with his parents and brother from their travels on the East Coast. They will stay at a hotel tonight, and then tomorrow's plan is for us to meet them at church and take them out on the boat. My husband has been feeling a little under the weather, though, and has a sore throat and a headache. "I think I'll be fine," he mumbles. "I'll just keep my distance from them in case I'm coming down with something."

> *"Are you tired? Worn out? Burned out on religion? Come to me. Get away with me and you'll recover your life. I'll show you how to take a real rest. Walk with me and work with me—watch how I do it. Learn the unforced rhythms of grace. I won't lay anything heavy or ill-fitting on you. Keep company with me and you'll learn to live freely and lightly." Matthew 11:28-30 The Message*

Sunday, June 12ᵗʰ, 2022

I WAKE UP TO MY normal nausea, swallow the lump in my throat, and will myself to put my feet on the ground. I step into the kitchen, turn the coffee pot on, and take some meds for nausea. I sit down with my coffee, sipping it, waiting for the medication to help with nausea. *Surely this will eventually go away, right?* It subsides some, and I go check on my husband. He groans from the bed and moans that he feels even worse. I rummage through our medicine cabinet to see if I can find something that may help. I come up with a cocktail of a few items and bring it back to him. "Take these and rest a bit longer. I'll get the boys to church and tell the exchange student's family that you've got a bit of a headache and need to get the boat ready, and that's the reason for your absence from church." He takes the meds, thanks me, and lies back down.

I arrive at church a little early with the two boys in tow, a miracle really with how slow these two move in the mornings. I immediately spot the exchange student and his family and head over to greet them. It really is amazing that they had the opportunity to come and meet us. We chat outside the church, and I explain the situation with my husband, then we head inside where I introduce them to several people.

About halfway through the service, my phone vibrates with a message. It's from my husband. "I can't do this. I have a fever now and can't stop throwing up. I feel horrible. There's no way I can go out on the boat today. I'm so sorry."

My mind immediately begins to try to come up with a contingency plan. I send texts to a couple of my brothers and my father-in-law to see if they may be able to take us out on the boat today. I also try a friend. It's a no-go on all those options. *Dang it!* They're only here for today. My daughter and her husband are supposed to be joining us on the lake, and I text her about the situation. "I've ordered a couple of party trays from Subway. Can you go and pick those up and bring them to the house? We can meet up there and figure out what we're going to do."

The service ends and I wonder if they noticed I spent nearly half the service on my phone. We step outside. The exchange student has met a girl who has been trying to learn Japanese, and they're chatting. I turn to his father, "Well, we have a bit of a situation." He peers at me attentively. His

English is very good. "One of the reasons my husband didn't come this morning is he wasn't feeling very well. He was hoping with some meds and rest, he would feel better, but he sent me a message saying that he now has a fever and is throwing up. I'm not able to launch the boat on my own, so unfortunately, I think that option is out."

The father's expression changes to a concerned one. "You don't need to worry about anything. We can find something to do. You can go take care of your husband if you need to."

"No, no, no. He'll be just fine. Our concern is exposing you to whatever he has. You know COVID is running rampant again, and we certainly don't need you guys popping a positive test trying to get home if that's what this is. My daughter is picking up some sandwiches for us and bringing them back to the house. We can go eat lunch there, outside if you prefer. My husband will stay in the bedroom, and we'll decide what to do. I'm just so sorry the lake is not going to work out."

"No worries. Sometimes, plans must change. I do hope your husband is okay. We will follow you to the house."

We arrive at the house, and I begin getting the sandwiches ready to be served while the exchange student shows his family around the house and the room that's been his for the past year. We decide to take the sandwiches and chips outside to eat on the porch. We're having a great time, visiting and laughing as we share stories. He has a fantastic family.

I slip inside to check on my husband. I find him in his office, crying. I sit down next to him and rub his back. "Why does it seem like nothing can go right?!" he sobs. My husband is not a crier, so I know this has gotten to him. "We've been planning this visit with his family for months and I just happen to get sick *the day* they come?!"

"It's going to be okay," I assure him. "We've decided to go downtown, walk the Promenade, shop, and go up in the mountain tower. Then, if they're up to it and it's not too terribly hot, I'll take them out to Garvan Gardens." I give him a reassuring squeeze and head back outside.

We spend several hours in the downtown area, and everyone enjoys themselves, even though it's pretty hot. They opt to go back to their hotel to rest rather than go to the Gardens. They'll come back to the house tonight for dinner.

They come back for dinner, and we discuss the next day's logistics. They must go get tested for COVID first thing in the morning and then will come here for breakfast, pack up, and head to the airport. Their son is scheduled to return home separately on Thursday.

"LORD, our Lord, how majestic is your name in all the earth! You have set your

glory in the heavens. Through the praise of children and infants you have established a stronghold against your enemies, to silence the foe and the avenger. When I consider your heavens, the work of your fingers, the moon and the stars, which you have set in place, what is mankind that you are mindful of them, human beings that you care for them? You have made them a little lower than the angels and crowned them with glory and honor. You made them rulers over the works of your hands; you put everything under their feet: all flocks and herds, and the animals of the wild, the birds in the sky, and the fish in the sea, all that swim the paths of the seas. LORD, our Lord, how majestic is your name in all the earth!" Psalm 8 NIV

Wednesday, June 15th, 2022

I WAKE TO AN EMAIL from my attorney that the request for a continuance has been denied and we're still on for the 27th. My pulse quickens. I had thought it would end up continued. He had a valid reason for asking. Why would they deny my request for a continuance but approve the continuance of the retrial? The retrial was supposed to happen last week, but it's been continued to some unknown date at this time. They've already done the trial once; everyone should have what they need to go ahead and do it over. *Who knows how they decide things up there in those courtrooms?* I begin sending out messages to people who have told me they want to come, telling them that it's still on for the 27th.

My husband is angry and creates a public Facebook post that in part reads:

> My wife was summoned to the courthouse on May 11th not knowing that she was about to be placed on trial. On May 11th, my wife was viciously slandered by an attorney and ridiculed mercilessly by a judge without representation. My wife was convicted without even knowing she was being charged.
>
> She was not read any rights. She was not given a chance at a defense. She was not given the opportunity for legal counsel. She was not allowed to speak. What is even more interesting is the individual juror who brought the complaint against her has remained nameless. In talking with several legal professionals, never in the history of Garland County has a juror come back after a unanimous decision and complained about another juror! Why did this juror complain?
>
> Did this juror not get his or her way in deliberations? What happened to proper "due process" in our legal system?
>
> Now, on June 27th, at 10:00 a.m., my wife will be back in the same judge's courtroom for her "sentencing." We've obtained legal counsel, but have been told to expect jail time. My wife was not granted a continuance for the June 27th date even though requested documents

for my wife's case have not been provided by the court after requests over three weeks ago.

My wife is no longer on Facebook as a way to protect herself, as her name was made public. The last month has been an incredibly trying time for my wife as I've watched her physical, mental, and emotional health struggle. My wife continues to tirelessly volunteer hours of her time each week to help foster kids and other vulnerable and disabled children and adults in our community.

She is an amazing mother to five children by birth and adoption. She is a "mother" to many others who have come into and out of our home throughout the years. I could go on, but hopefully, you got the picture.

If you know my wife, if you know our family, we are asking for support in the courtroom. We need your presence. We are clinging to the promise in Romans 8:28, "We know that all things work together for the good of those who love God: those who are called according to His purpose" [HCSB]. Will you pray that with us?

My wife's favorite color is purple. Will you join me in wearing purple on June 27th at 10:00 a.m. and feel free to join us in the courtroom.

His post is shared sixty-plus times in a matter of hours, and then I get a message from my attorney that it needs to be taken down. He reluctantly complies.

> *"Consider it a sheer gift, friends, when tests and challenges come at you from all sides. You know that under pressure, your faith-life is forced into the open and shows its true colors. So don't try to get out of anything prematurely. Let it do its work, so you become mature and well-developed, not deficient in any way." James 1:2-4 The Message*

Thursday, June 16th, 2022

OUR EXCHANGE STUDENT IS RETURNING to Japan today. My husband and I head out in the morning to take him to the airport. Because he's a minor, they allow us to take him to his gate. We stay with him until they begin lining up to board the plane. We then awkwardly stand and start to give our goodbyes. It's very possible we may never see him again. He reaches his hand out to shake mine, but I push it aside and wrap him in a hug. I pull his face back and kiss him on the forehead. He laughs nervously, and my husband tells me to quit embarrassing him. I tell him to message us when he arrives at his connection and to stay in touch. He promises he will, and we watch him enter the gateway ramp. I'll miss that kid.

We head back to Hot Springs for a closing on the house we have found for our daughter and son-in-law. The original closing was set for the 27th and I had reminded my realtor that date wouldn't work. Managing to get it closed this fast is amazing. My realtor tells me again that she plans to be at court on the 27th. I thank her. I'm thankful my daughter will now have a place close by.

Since we didn't get to go out on the boat last weekend, my husband decides to take the rest of the day off and we head to the lake. We pack snacks and drinks and enjoy a boat ride. We find a quiet island to get out and just float for a while. Something about the sun and water is therapy for me. I take a deep breath in and exhale.

"You are my refuge and my shield; I have put my hope in your word." Psalm 119:114 NIV

Friday, June 17ᵗʰ, 2022

I RECEIVE AN EMAIL FROM the facility where my disabled son is staying, letting me know they're having a planning meeting for him on the 30ᵗʰ and need either me or my husband to attend or be available via phone. *Gosh, how to respond... "Well, I can't commit because I may be in jail"?* I feel like my life is on hold until I get this behind me. I tell them that I will try to make the trip there but, if I don't show, to call my husband's cell. That's the best I can do.

Today I have my first appointment back with my therapist. We start with the normal pleasantries, and then

I go ahead and dive into the whole story of the past couple of months. She has the same reaction everyone does: flabbergasted, dumbfounded, and confused. I'm stumbling through my words and crying by the time I get to the end. "All I've ever tried to do is do right by people, you know? And now I'm responsible for this?!"

I get home and take a minute to examine my eye in the bathroom. I had thought it was getting better, but it seems to be flaring back up. *Ugh*, always something.

> *"'For I know the plans I have for you,'*
> *declares the LORD, 'plans to prosper you and*
> *not to harm you, plans to give you hope and*
> *a future.'" Jeremiah 29:11 NIV*

Sunday, June 19th, 2022

I RETIRE TO MY CHAIR with my dogs early tonight. It's one of those evenings where the weight of everything is just too heavy for me to read my book. *What if I do go to jail?* I think about all the things I do daily, the people I take care of, my clients, my boys, and my husband, and the tears fall. My husband and one son are at the gym, and my other son is up in his room. I send him a text, "Wanna come down and hang out?"

"Why?" he responds.

"Just wanted someone to talk to."

He appears in the living room, takes a seat on the couch, and glances over at me. He then sighs, gets up, and meanders over to me. "Come here," he whispers as he sits on the edge of the chair and pulls me close to embrace me.

This one always knows when I'm upset and struggling, and for some reason, I've always been able to cry with him and share my hurts and heart.

"Everything is going to be okay. It's all going to work out and you're going to be fine," he says softly as he rubs my back.

"Will you come to court with me?" I cry.

He waits a while to respond and pulls back from me. "I can't do that, Mom. I just can't. If that judge starts talking bad to you and puts you in jail—man, I just don't know. I think I'll end up in jail too. It just won't be good."

I wipe my tears away, blow my nose, and tell him I understand. He gives me another hug and wanders back upstairs. I've been through so much with that one. I love him with a fierce love, but there are so many red flags that he's not going to be able to overcome the trauma he's been through. I don't dismiss the progress he's made, though; man, has he made progress. We used to not go a week without a new hole in a wall or a piece of property destroyed. Still, if he doesn't do the earnest work necessary to heal, I know he's going to be headed for a difficult life. I hope the day doesn't come when my love for him will mean "letting him go." I've learned that letting go is one of the most painful things required by love: continuing to give of yourself when the person persists in destructive patterns is only to make you feel better, not help the other person. Love creates boundaries, not just for yourself, but for the other person as well.

"You've kept track of my every toss and turn through the sleepless nights, each tear entered in your ledger, each ache written in your book." Psalm 56:8 The Message

Monday, June 20th, 2022

IT'S ONE WEEK TILL COURT, and my attorney wants to meet with me and my husband to be sure we know what to expect. He ushers us into his office, and we sit at the conference table. "Do you guys have any questions for me?" he starts.

"Do you really not think there's a defamation case against the defense attorney that can be made?"

"Not really. I mean, you're welcome to check with someone else, though."

"And you don't think it would be beneficial for any witnesses to speak on my behalf?"

"Katrina, just them showing up in support of you is going to speak volumes. There's rarely any sense in having a bunch of people stand up there to say, 'You're a good person.' Good people make mistakes."

"The owner of my firm is willing to say he made me the Chief Compliance Officer of our firm *because* of my attention to rules. Surely that would lend itself to showing I'm not someone who would maliciously, intentionally, willfully break a rule?!"

"And you didn't intentionally break a rule, did you?"

"No, but obviously I did, and see what it's caused!" I choke out. "I set out to do the best job I could as a juror, and now everything is a mess." The tears keep coming and my voice cracks, but I push forward. "Do you have any idea the hell all of this has been for me?! Furthermore, how are they going to get people to show up for jury duty if this can be the result? I know it's already a challenge to get juries."

The demeanor of my attorney softens. "Katrina, you're not a bad person and you're a dream of a juror, especially for the defense. You're someone who can see someone as innocent until they're proven guilty. Most people can't do that. You did something that we all know *lots* of jurors do. But yes, it is a bit of a quandary if this story gets out, especially if you go to jail."

"I'm just stupid enough to admit I attempted some research. God, I'm so dumb. I spent four days with that group of people and felt like they were nearly my best friends by the time it was over. A weakness I have. I make a statement, while in my emotions, that has no bearing on our deliberations and vote, and I enter an alternate reality. I just don't get it." My hands are shaking, and I reach for another tissue. Surely, he has people break down on him all the time, and that's why he keeps tissues on the table. He probably sees people at their lowest often.

"Katrina, this judge is going to want to know you've suffered for what you've done, and she's going to want an apology. Walk in there humble and apologetic, and I don't think you'll do jail time."

"Well, I've certainly suffered, and I tried to apologize at the last hearing, but she wouldn't let me get a word in edgewise. I was humble then, and she basically told me I make her sick to her stomach."

We meet for over an hour and a half. He gives me an idea of some of the questions he or the judge may ask. I decide I'm going to go home and type up answers. I tell him I won't bring a prepared statement, but I feel like I need something to rehearse. We trudge out of his office, and it's already dinner time. I'm emotionally spent. "I don't think I can pull off a dinner tonight," I tell my husband.

"Don't worry about dinner. We'll figure it out."

"How long, LORD? Will you forget me forever? How long will you hide your face from me? How long must I wrestle with my thoughts and day after day have sorrow in my heart? How long will my enemy triumph over me? Look on me and answer, LORD my God. Give light to my eyes, or I will sleep in death, and my enemy will say, 'I have overcome him,' and my foes will rejoice when I fall. But I trust in your unfailing love; my heart rejoices in your salvation. I will sing the LORD's praise, for he has been good to me." Psalm 13 NIV

Wednesday, June 22nd, 2022

I HAVE AN EXTREMELY BUSY day today, but it starts with me checking my email and seeing my attorney's office has sent the rest of the court transcripts we had requested. *Now*, the court decides to send them. *Good grief.* Oh, and there's a bill with it for $738 dollars, of course. That brings the total amount spent on this nonsense up to $3,635.70. I add "take the check to the attorney's office" to my list of things to do for the day. I save the file and set it to print. I don't have time to read it now but will prepare that as my evening activity. Should be fun reading…

After a full day and dinner, I head to my office to start reading the transcripts. I'll have to do my evening reading here rather than in my chair. As I start to read, I realize this certainly isn't going to be relaxing reading. The main transcript is from the voir dire part of the hearing. It's 175 pages long and I read every word. My emotions are all over the place as I relive that day in court; my anxiety has me rocking as I read each page. Reliving it from the perspective I have now, knowing what this is the beginning of for me, is a little overwhelming.

When I finish, my heart is thudding with anger. The voir dire transcript confirms that never was it asked if anyone knew the judge personally. Neither was an even more general question about "knowing anyone in the court proceedings" ever asked. There were only specific questions regarding specific individuals, with the judge not being included. Furthermore, the defense attorney never asked *any* "do you know this person or these people…" questions. The guy lied, and it makes me angry.

My attorney has said that, although the defense attorney made a big deal out of me not revealing during voir dire that

I knew the judge, it's me looking the victim up in Court Connect that the judge in my sentencing hearing is going to focus on. Yet, as I was confident about, the transcript also shows that the victim was never mentioned during voir dire. No one is asked if they knew him, and he isn't identified as a party to the case.

I need to pack it up and go to bed. I'm going to need something to help me sleep, so I head over to the medicine cabinet. *Breathe in…breathe out.*

> *"I will refresh the weary and satisfy the faint." Jeremiah 31:25 NIV*

Thursday, June 23rd, 2022

I START THE DAY EARLY with a drive with my son to the courthouse in a neighboring town. He must go and show that he has completed all the requirements from the ticket he received for the last wreck he was in. He's done everything he's supposed to, and I know the judge is going to go easy on him and dismiss the ticket. My son is still nervous and bites and picks at a couple of his fingernails till they're bleeding. He asks nervous questions about what things mean as other people are called up and dealt with by the judge. His name is eventually called and, since he's still a minor, I approach with him.

"Let's see," starts the judge. "Looks like you paid the court fee when you were here last. You were supposed to complete a day of community service and go to defensive driving. Have you completed those?"

"Yes sir." He starts to lift his completion certificates to show the judge.

"No. No, I don't need that. I see here that you got both of those taken care of. Because you did everything I asked and you showed up today, I'm going to dismiss this. I need you to be more careful and pay attention."

"Thank you, sir, and I will. I haven't even been allowed to drive since the wreck."

The bailiff directs us over to a table for us to sign some papers while the judge calls the next person up.

My son is quiet during most of the drive home, and I hope I don't have to spend other days in court with him. I focus on just getting home. This has taken nearly half the day, and I have so much to get done before Monday.

Before I jump into all the other tasks of the day, there's something more important I need to take care of. On September 7th of last year, my husband's younger brother succumbed to a long battle against alcohol. Today is his birthday. I know it will be a hard day for his mom and many in the family, including the children he left behind. I swing by a floral shop and pick up a bouquet and make sure it has sunflowers in it, my mother-in-law's favorite. "Are you home?" I ask in a quick text to her.

"Yes, for the next thirty minutes," she responds.

"I'm going to swing by really quick."

I arrive at her home and let myself in. I find her in the kitchen and hand the flowers over. "I know what day it is, and I knew it would probably be a hard one."

"Come here and give me a hug!" she exclaims. "They're beautiful! Thank you so much!"

This woman has been through so much with her kids and grandchildren. I think I've only seen her cry once, but I know she must have cried rivers for them. I know for certain she's prayed on her knees and probably soaked the Scriptures with her tears. Yet, she had to bury her youngest child. It just doesn't seem fair.

My husband's sister has also had a problem with alcohol for most of her life. It's driven a wedge between me and the family. As far as I'm aware, she's been sober since the death of her brother. I'm thankful for that. She is an amazing soul when she's doing well, but when she's not, it's bad, really bad. After a couple of decades of not knowing what I'd get from her, I had to bow out.

So, my mother-in-law and I don't always see eye-to-eye on how to love a person who's causing damage to themselves and others, but I've never doubted for a second that she loves and loves strong. I have different philosophies, but I'm not batting one thousand on correcting poor choices in my children either.

I worry about my husband's nieces and nephews; they've experienced so much trauma, and the evidence of that is so clear. Can they be healed and not continue the cycle with children of their own? Absolutely! They will have to be intentional and pursue it with perseverance, though.

"Train up a child in the way he should go, even when he grows older he will not abandon it." Proverbs 22:6 NASB

Friday, June 24th, 2022

I'VE STARTED PUTTING TOGETHER A list for my husband in case I do end up in jail: instructions, phone numbers, passwords, etc. My attorney seemed confident I wouldn't go to jail, but I would rather be prepared. I also get with my colleagues and let them know about the clients who need things taken care of in the next couple of weeks or so. They're more than supportive. I jot down a note to change my voicemail the morning of court to direct people to either the office or my husband, depending on if it's business or personal. *I should also set a "vacation reply" on my email,* I think, and create a note. I then make notes of the medications that each of our boys takes, and when, for my husband. Then I figure I'll go fill up the medication boxes for the lady I help. I've gotten her into a facility that administers her medications, but I still fill up her boxes every two weeks. I haven't told this lady about the possibility of jail time. It would upset her too much. I compose a note of her various appointments for the next couple of weeks and add it to my husband's list; he will have to get in touch with the director of the facility and see if they can take her to those appointments. *Good grief! Why am I having to do all this?! One foot in front of the other, Katrina. Breathe in, breathe out.*

I stare down at my tattoos. I've already decided what I want to get next when all this is behind me: a phoenix bird, on my shoulder, rising from the ashes. I want it in purple and teal. I had asked when my artist could get me in, and he said not till November. I decide to check in with him again and see if he's had any cancelations by chance.

"I have a spot open; I can fit you in on the 28th," he responds.

Hmmm, I think. *Maybe it's a sign that I won't be going to jail.* "I'll take it," I reply. "I have court the day before, but my attorney thinks I won't do jail time. If I don't show, you'll know why."

> *"He brought me up from a desolate pit, out of the muddy clay, and set my feet on a rock, making my steps secure." Psalm 40:2 HSCB*

ONE OF THE THINGS I'VE splurged on myself for years now is getting my nails done. I've had the same nail tech for probably five years. At this point, he's like a friend and a therapist. He doesn't do appointments on Sundays, only walk-ins. I know he stays busy, and I don't have time to wait. I send him a message and ask if he can make an exception for me this one time. He tells me he can get me in, and I head over there.

I always let him do whatever he wants with my nails. This time, I tell him what I want, though. I sift through all the colors and pick out a purple and a teal. "I want these," I say while pointing to them. "And then add some sort of sparkle or shine to them."

"Okay, Miss Katrina." He gives instructions to another worker, in Vietnamese, and he comes back with the colors I've asked for. "Why you want Sunday appointment? You never come on Sundays."

"Well," I begin. "I have court tomorrow. I want fresh nails and I want them to match the dress I'll be wearing."

"You have court? Is everything okay?" he asks while taking a minute to peek up at me.

"No, everything is not okay. There's a possibility I may go to jail."

"Who go to jail?"

"Me, I may go to jail," I manage to get out as a tear slips from my eye.

"Oh, Miss Katrina! I'm so sorry. I feel bad now." He stares back down at my hands and continues to quietly work on my nails. My tears are falling freely now, silently. "I don't understand how you go to jail, Miss Katrina. Is someone mad at you?"

"Something like that. It's long and complicated. For whatever reason, I felt like I needed fresh nails for it. Kind of silly but here I am."

"It's no problem." He's finishing them up and checking them again to make sure he doesn't need to fix any mistakes. "I hope you win, and I see you again soon."

"Me too." I pay, leave him a tip, and slip out.

> *"I love you, GOD—you make me strong. GOD is bedrock under my feet, the castle in which I live, my rescuing knight. My God—the high crag where I run for dear life, hiding behind the boulders, safe in the granite hideout. I sing to GOD, the Praise-Lofty, and find myself safe and saved."*
> *Psalm 18:1-3 The Message*

Monday, June 27th, 2022

I WAKE IN THE MORNING without the normal nausea. *Strange,* I think to myself. *I expected it to be worse this morning.* Throughout my morning coffee, shower, and getting ready, I don't feel the anxiousness that I expected. As I sit down to go over my notes on how to respond to questions, an emotion does surface. Anger. I'm angry with the entire situation. Angry I'm having to do this. I pace around my office. This is not the emotion my attorney wants me to bring into the courtroom. I don't always control my emotions well, though. There's a knock at the door and I see it's my friend bringing me a pair of shoes to wear. I didn't have any I could settle on.

"How are you doing?" she asks.

"You know, I'm not like I thought I would be. I'm just angry now, *really* angry. You'll have to pray that the Lord will control my emotions and my tongue."

"I'll do that," she responds, "and I'll see you there."

She leaves and I go back to pacing. One son has already gone to work, and I go upstairs to wake the other one. He sees I'm dressed for court, wearing my purple dress, and wishes me luck.

It's time to go, so I go get my husband and tell him I'm ready. He's very somber. He's quiet as he puts his jacket on and we walk toward the garage. We sit in the car, he puts his hand on my knee, tries to say a prayer, and then the sobs emerge from him. "I'm so scared of what's going to happen to you, Katrina!"

"You've got to calm down! Everything is going to be fine, no matter what happens. There are worse things we could be going through. You know that, don't you?"

He wipes his eyes. "I know. You're right." He backs the car out of the garage, but he stays in a somber mood on the way. As for me, I feel like the weight is about to be lifted from me.

As we pull into the parking lot, my entire office family has just parked and is getting out of their cars. They stroll toward me, all in their purple. I'm so humbled.

We head to the courtroom, and I'm greeted by others who have come to support me, also wearing purple. My attorney is waiting on me. He tells me we will wait till most all my supporters have arrived, as close to 10:00 a.m. as possible, before we walk in so we can all go in together.

I zig-zag my way to various friends and family members and conjure up small talk. The minutes seem to be dragging on like hours. The anxiety is finally kicking in. My mouth is getting dry, my legs are shaky, and I need to be able to sit down.

Ten o'clock finally arrives and my attorney leads us all into the courtroom. We look like quite the entourage. I think there are thirty or so people with me, but I don't take the time to count. I take a seat at the defense table with my attorney. I survey the room and, when my eyes land on the jury box, realize that, ironically, the defendant is here. I didn't realize she would be here, and I ask my attorney about it. He tells me that he didn't expect her, either, but that it makes sense since it's regarding her trial.

We then sit back and wait, and wait. Fifteen minutes go by, and everyone is getting restless. The bailiff then approaches and announces that the hold-up is because court must wait for the defense attorney to arrive, as he wasn't aware he was supposed to be here. He tells us it will be thirty to forty-five more minutes. There's an audible, exasperated sigh from everyone and quite a bit of grumbling.

Now I feel sick to my stomach. All these people have taken time out of their day, and now more of it will be wasted. I chat with various people, but for the most part, I just sit. I notice a man I recognize sitting in one of the rows, but I can't place him. I'd seen my attorney speak with him, so I ask who he is.

"He's another attorney," my attorney states.

"Why's he here?" I ask, confused.

"He's just curious. As I said, this hasn't ever happened before. He just wants to see how it plays out."

"Ah yes, of course. I'm the unicorn. You know, I had a dream the other night about this hearing, and I showed up in a unicorn costume." I've had all kinds of dreams the past month and this is one of the funnier ones.

My attorney laughs, "I guess you should have come to jury selection in the unicorn costume."

I notice my husband sitting next to a reporter from the newspaper. My husband is filling the reporter's ears while the reporter takes notes. Two of my friends have gone over there to apparently supervise. *Great*, I think, *no telling what kind of story he's getting.*

By now, a couple of people have had to leave due to other obligations. I'm starting to seethe that we're being forced to wait on this guy. Then my oldest brother stands up and comes toward the wall separating us. I can tell he's fighting back tears. I approach him and he reaches out his arms to hug me. "I can't wait on this jerk any longer," he says through a clenched jaw.

"It's okay, bro. I love you." He quickly turns to leave. I go back to watching the clock.

Finally, at a little past 11:00 a.m., the defense attorney strides in. There's an audible "booo" from my supporters, and I shake my head but can't help but grin. *Yep, those are my people.*

The defense attorney strides toward his client, and the bailiff lets the judge know he's here. About five minutes later, we all hear, "All rise! Court is now in session."

I stand. *Here we go,* I think. The courtroom is cold, but I'm perspiring. The judge enters and tells us we can be seated.

After being sworn in and some of the necessary disclosures are made at the beginning, the State begins by wanting to admit as evidence the transcript of the hearing from May 11th when I was found to be in contempt of court. At this point, my attorney stands and says that I would object to that. *Wait?! I do?* I'm thinking to myself. He continues, "Obviously in that matter, there could be some testimony from other individuals that could be held against her in this case. She had no right to confront them and no right to ask any questions of them. Obviously, that's in direct violation of the U.S. Constitution— being able to hold that against her, not allowing her to confront witnesses who would be used against her in this case."

The judge turns towards the prosecutor for the State, "Is there any reason why those witnesses are not here today? Are they prevented from being here for any reason?"

The prosecutor stands and stumbles with her words for a moment. "No, they're not. The State's further comment regarding that is that Juror #11 is not charged with any criminal offense. Those Constitutional guarantees are based on a criminal offense, and at this point in time, she's not charged with any criminal offense."

The judge is clearly irritated. "Well, she's charged with contempt of court, which is a criminal penalty, and it has to be proven according to due process. So, I'm going to continue this hearing so that the State can have those witnesses here in light of the fact that Ms. Robertson has objected on the record to that. This hearing will be continued for one month."

Things are happening so fast. I want to grasp my attorney by the arm and tell him to say that never mind, we don't object. *Is that an option?! I don't want this continued!* I would love to have Juror #8 questioned but not at the expense of dragging this out. It's too late. The judge, my attorney, and the State are already discussing dates. The room is spinning, and then I hear "August the 3rd, 2022, at 1:30 p.m. in this courtroom." And then the hearing is over.

My husband stands and asks loudly, "What just happened?!"

People begin to stand, trying to figure out what to do next. Some begin to exit. I wait, thinking I need to talk to my attorney before leaving. Most everyone has left, and I approach my attorney. "I guess I can leave, and we will be in touch?"

"Yes. I'm sorry. I should have warned you that this was a possibility. I knew the State wouldn't be calling any witnesses."

I tread out of the courtroom to where a handful of my supporters have gathered. My emotions finally hit me, and I put my head in my hands and sob. "I'm so sorry, guys! I just wanted this over!"

Many come over and try to comfort me and we head down the stairs together.

I get home, change out of my dress, and hang it up, knowing I will now have to put it back on in about five weeks. I try to lie down, but my head is spinning, and my phone won't stop buzzing. I give up, answer some texts, and try to act normal. I take the vacation replies off my email and voicemail and figure out what I'm going to cook for dinner.

"Blessed is the one who perseveres under trial because, having stood the test, that person will receive the crown of life that the Lord has promised to those who love him."
James 1:12 NIV

Tuesday, June 28th, 2022

I WAKE IN THE MORNING to read the newspaper's article, "Hearing Postponed on Contempt Charge in Murder Mistrial." *Awesome*, I think as I scan through the article. It's a fair piece, and I like that it's mentioned that we were delayed over an hour while waiting on the defense attorney. The end of it includes a few comments from my husband. He mentions the defense attorney making a big deal out of my relationship with the judge but lying about the question ever being asked. He brags about me being a woman of character who fought for the defendant. The article then quotes him as saying, "She took her civic duty very seriously and just wanted to do what was right."

My attorney then calls me and tells me that my husband should not have made the statements to the newspaper. "All statements should go through me, and at this point, you don't need to be saying anything."

I'm frustrated. "Well, when exactly do I get to share my side of the story?" I ask.

"After your hearing, Katrina. Until then, no statements to the paper. No Facebook posts."

I feel defeated, but I tell him we'll cooperate. I pass the word along to my husband. *I swear, I can never do anything right.*

I had cleared today, and most of the week, of any appointments. I still have a list of things I need to take care of, and a webinar for work to listen to, but I decide to take a couple of hours to read by the pool at my mother-in-law's. I've been finding time to do this at least once a week, and I've gotten a nice tan in the process. I've put together a playlist of songs that have been an encouragement to me, and I play them while I read and float. It's been therapy for me.

I still have my tattoo appointment. I send him a message and let him know I'll be there. A friend is meeting me there. As I'm coming in the door, my tattoo artist meets me with a grin, holding his phone up. "Look what just came up on my newsfeed!"

He shows me his phone with the summary of the newspaper article highlighted. "It knew you were coming!" he laughs. "I need to hear the story now!"

I settle into the chair as my friend arrives. I've brought my speaker to play my "therapy" playlist while he works. I tell him about the hearing or lack thereof, and that now I have to stress over it for five more weeks. He finishes my phoenix and I admire it. "I love it," I say.

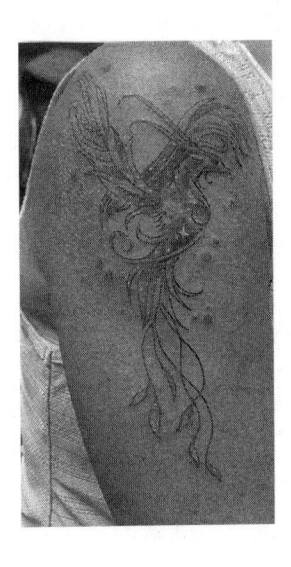

My friend and I head down the street for some drinks and cheese dip. We enjoy each other's company as we talk about this crazy ride called life.

When I get home, I decide I'm reactivating my Facebook. I do so and create a post with a picture of my fresh tattoo.

> *I'm back*! Almost two months away from laughing and crying with my friends and experiencing life with them "virtually" is too long. Times are hard, folks—*really* hard, and I just needed to take a moment to step back and breathe. I'm not going to hide any longer in my pain and suffering. I never have, have I?! Some people like my openness, honesty, and vulnerability—others not so much. I can't share many of the details of the current battle but most of you already know and you know it's not over. But, like the Phoenix Bird, I *will* rise! This is just a mythical bird, but it's a symbol of hope, renewal, rebirth, immortality, resurrection, solitude, and grace. Just like the phoenix emerges from its ashes, so can man after devastation and loss. It's a symbol of hope and urges us to fight on!
>
> So sister girl,
>
> When you're mentally, physically, and emotionally exhausted, through Him, you can rise!
>
> When you feel like you can't function, through Him, you can rise!
>
> When you make a mistake that causes grief to others, you can rise!

When you're misunderstood and good intentions go awry, you can rise!

When it's not a big thing you're facing, but just *all* the hard little things *Every*. Single. Day, you can rise!

When you're amid injustices and things just don't seem fair, you can rise!

Even if it's death you're facing, through Him, you *will* rise!

Now, this doesn't mean you will always *feel* like you will rise. I can assure you, that will not be the case. Sometimes, the emotions are so heavy that they feel crushing. A quote [from the book *The Boy, the Mole, the Fox and the Horse* says], "Sometimes just getting up and carrying on is brave and magnificent."

So, carry on, rise, and be magnificent, friends!

I receive a Facebook message from the very first CASA kid I ever had. "Love the new tattoo! But what's wrong?? Are you okay?"

I type out the shortest summary I can to her, and she sends a response. "Pardon my French but...*Holy shit*! You're literally one of the best, if not the best person I know. Of all people to get wrapped up in some crazy stuff like this...I'm so sorry. I wish there was something I could do."

I tell her she's welcome to come to court if she just happens to be in town then.

"I wish I could! I know you have the world rooting and supporting you though! As you should!"

I'm proud of this one. She has come *so* far from where she was when I met her as a struggling 16-year-old.

Me at her graduation after getting her
GED in the top of her class.

"Pure and undefiled religion before our God and Father is this: to look after orphans and widows in their distress and to keep oneself unstained by the world." James 1:27 HCSB

Wednesday, June 29th, 2022

I DECIDE I'M GOING TO do a Facebook post each day until court, thirty-five days away, with a link to one of the songs on the playlist I had created for encouragement. I start out with this one...

"Music and scripture are two of the therapies that keep me grounded. In thirty-five days, I will go to court and whatever the judge decides, I will *rise*. So, for the next thirty-five days, I wanted to share a song that has been there for me and possibly a scripture too. Today's song goes with my theme. 'Rise' by Shawn McDonald. If you're struggling and overwhelmed, give it a listen."

The song talks about rising from the ashes, from trouble, and that you're able to do this because He is inside of us. Sometimes our hearts and souls are crushed, and we can't find any hope, but we hold on to the truth in spite of what we're feeling.

> "GOD's loyal love couldn't have run out, his merciful love couldn't have dried up. They're created new every morning. How great your faithfulness! I'm sticking with GOD (I say it over and over). He's all I've got left." Lamentations 3:22-24 The Message

Thursday, June 30th, 2022

TODAY IS THE DAY OF the meeting for my disabled son at the facility. I've emailed them and let them know I will be able to attend. It's a little over a two-hour drive and the meeting is at 10:00 a.m., so I get on the road by 7:30 a.m. to allow for a stop if needed. I have quite a bit of stuff to take to him, so I have the car loaded up. I'm numb on the drive there. I'm not sure how I'm going to handle seeing him. This one I'd probably fought for more persistently than many others combined. Absolute heartbreak is all I received in return for my fight. I feel like a failure all the way around and wonder why God even picked me to advocate for him.

I arrive at the facility and weave my way around buildings. It's a massive campus with lots of buildings. I find where I'm to check in and I'm directed to the building I need to go to. My pulse has picked up, and I'm getting nervous now. My nervous emotion has me feeling even more guilt. *Why can't you be happy to see him, Katrina?* I beat myself up a little more and enter the building for the meeting. I quickly spot him, sitting at a table; I put my happy face on and go over to greet him. It's an awkward greeting. He smiles a little but then hangs his head and averts his eyes. This is the same type of greeting he's given me when I've visited him at other facilities over the years, including while he was stuck in the ER at the local hospital. Yes, he's intellectually disabled, but I believe he knows how deeply he has hurt me. I still feel shame when he doesn't show excitement to see me. He shows excitement with other family members, but not me. I've not hidden any of my hurt, anger, and devastation from him, though.

I take a seat at the table. There are probably ten or so individuals there to go over his plan of care, progress, concerns, goals, etc. The woman to my right opens the meeting with, "Noah is so lucky to have you. It's obvious you're such an advocate for him. Most of our residents don't have that."

I nearly choke and can't respond. *Lucky to have me? Why would she say that? If he were lucky, I would have been able to keep him out of a facility, right?* I swallow hard and blink to keep the tears from coming.

The meeting progresses, and they tell me they believe he's doing well there, is making progress, and is a good fit to continue to stay. I'm a little surprised because of some of the incident reports I've received, but I remind myself that they deal with some of the hardest of the hard there. I give them lots of ideas on things that help de-escalate him, entertain him, motivate him, etc. They all take notes. We wrap the meeting up, and I tell him I'll take him to lunch. He has relaxed during the meeting, and his normal chatty self is back.

I meet him over at his "cottage" and meet a few of the other young men who live with him. We unload all the items I've brought for him. He's especially excited about his fishing stuff. He then tells me he wants Mexican for lunch, so we load up and I do a quick search on my phone for a Mexican place. I locate one, hit "go," and we head that way.

We enjoy our meal, have a conversation, and he FaceTimes my husband. Once we've completely cleaned our plates, I pay our bill, and we head back to the facility. He's chatty all the way back, telling me *all* the things about *all* the people. I'm quiet for the most part. My emotions are starting to get strong.

I get him back to his cottage, give him a hug, tell him to be good, and head back to my car. I now have a two-hour drive by myself to process everything in my head. I don't get far down the curvy roads before I'm overwhelmed with emotion. Sobs come from deep in my gut, and I beat the steering wheel with my hand. "Why didn't you fix this, God?!" I scream. I need to find a place to pull over.

I find a spot to pull over, roll my windows down, turn the car off, and lean my seat back. I want to curl up into the fetal position and cry it out. I think back over the past nine years. My heart is broken, my spirit crushed, and my soul hurt.

In 2013, I stumbled on a video of a young boy who was in foster care and needed a family. They "interviewed" him at the Purple Cow. I went on a mission to find him and help him. I fought with DHS and the State for eighteen months before they let me bring him home and adopt him. On December 16th, 2014, the adoption was finalized, and I had big dreams for him.

He can bring joy to the people he's around, and he finds joy in simple things. In fact, I had the Hebrew word for "Joy" tattooed on my back as my "word" for him. Then, we found out the demons of his past had risen their heads when we discovered he had been molesting a nephew. The grief of that realization brought torrents of sorrow. Despite the anger, bitterness, and questions this caused for me with God, we held on tight to him. We *knew* we could still help him. We only needed to watch him closer.

Then, he molested another nephew. My brother called and said he needed to come and talk to me in person. He came to my house, and with love in his voice, explained what his then four-year-old son told him had happened. I listened on trembling legs. My brother wasn't angry, but we knew now we must watch him even closer.

Next, there was a call to the police, and he was taken to jail for molesting a *stranger* in a *public* park. He was with a caregiver, but the caregiver had gotten distracted, and my son took the opportunity to drag a kid behind a building and molest him. An eyewitness took pictures before she called the police. Going over that police report, forcing myself to view the pictures, and then sitting in a court hearing for six hours, ended with me in the hospital with acute appendicitis.

Then we *doubled down* the supervision. I talked to the aides about what they were dealing with, a sexual predator. I began fighting on the state level, with DHS, with the governor, with DDS, with attorneys, etc., to try to get this addressed from a hormonal/medication level. We tried countless meds but during that time he had several incidents at school where hotline calls had to be made. He was also found repeatedly trying to "rape" the dog.

What forced him out of our home, and into facilities, was that we caught him molesting a brother. The courts then ordered him to a facility, which I knew wasn't a good fit, but it was our only option. It took a year for me to find a place that was more suitable for him, and it was in a state 1,500 miles away. This was only one of two facilities in the entire United States that would agree to take him. I thought *maybe* they could give him the right therapy, medication, something. I knew that he would only have a year there, and I would need that entire year to figure out a plan. During that year, he continued to sexually assault and choose staff whom he could be aggressive toward.

The solution for him that I came up with was to build a house next to ours, staffed with 24/7 aides to keep one-on-one supervision on him. That seemed like it might work. Then he turned eighteen and began to be even more aggressive because "he was eighteen and could do what he wanted."

He only had *one* opportunity to act out sexually and he took it—five minutes without me in the same room with him, and a dog available. He again showed his ability to plan and manipulate to take advantage of a situation. He even turned the TV down so he could hear if I were coming. Any time he felt like he'd gotten away with something, he was proud of it.

Then there was the problem with him continually being mean to the aides, scaring them, and running them off. He seemed proud when he "showed out" and bossed them around. He was getting braver with his aggression toward them and sneakier in making sure I wasn't home when he threatened and manipulated them. The anxiety I was facing began to start taking a toll on me physically. I was rapidly losing weight and my hair was falling out.

I was dealing with a raging kidney infection, from the stress, when he decided he would push the newest aide past her limits. I wasn't at home, and he knew that. I was watching him on the camera and told my husband he needed to go home and deal with him. My husband arrived and told the aide to go on home while he sat outside and tried to let our son get his "fit" out of his system. For an hour my husband sat there while my son yelled, screamed, cussed, and threw rocks. Then he started to act aggressively toward my husband, who locked himself in the cottage. That's when my son decided he would kick the door in to get to my husband. It was a metal, dead-bolted door that he kicked off the frame. Then I pulled up. I found my husband scared and sobbing while my son began to apologize profusely, stating he wouldn't do it again. I was done. Couldn't do it for one more minute of one more day. I made sure the police were on the way. And there began six months of him being either stuck in an ER, at a homeless shelter, or in jail until the State finally had this place for him.

As I sit here in the car in a gas station parking lot, I grieve the loss of all the dreams I had for him: to graduate high school, live as independently as possible, play on sports teams, and even have a job. I wonder if all my fighting had helped him in some way. *Would he have ended up on the streets or in jail? Would he have been taken advantage of, or would he have had access to people and kids he could hurt?* There's no way of knowing for sure. I do know I did all I could and have to accept that this is the best place for him and everyone else. I send a text to my husband, "On my way back. I don't think I'll be able to make this trip very often."

I get myself pulled together and go get some water inside the gas station I've been parked at. *There's no other choice but to keep going, right?* I put my playlist on in the car and sing along to find encouragement while I drive.

"GOD *proves to be good to the man who passionately waits, to the woman who diligently seeks. It's a good thing to quietly hope, quietly hope for help from* GOD. *It's a good thing when you're young to stick it out through the hard times." Lamentations 3:25-27 The Message*

Wednesday, July 6th, 2022

MY DAYS HAVE BEEN FULL with work, getting various people to doctor appointments, and helping the boys juggle their schedules. Today is no exception and starts with a drive to Benton to meet with a client. This client has been with me for a while, and I had just helped get him retired. Most of our communication has been via phone and email, so it is nice to get to meet with him face-to-face. I consider nearly all my clients friends, and this one is no exception. On the drive home, a message flashes on my dash that a text has come through from my mother-in-law to both me and my husband. I push the button for the text to be read to me. "Katrina is in the paper again, front page. The children of the victim are filing a wrongful death suit, but the article mentions Katrina as well." The message then indicates that she has sent an image.

The road seems to become uneven, and the air in the car gets thick. My pulse quickens, and I begin to scan for a place to pull over so I can look at the article. Fortunately, there's a gas station right up ahead, and I pull in. I don't know why the anxiety has hit me so strongly. My hands are shaking as I pull my phone out of the console to read the article. It only briefly mentions me, but I feel like I'm forever going to be "that horrible person who caused a mistrial." My mouth starts to water, as well as my eyes, and I can feel the lump in my throat rising. I open my car door, afraid I won't be able to hold it in. I had just had lunch with my client. I take a sip of water and tell myself to breathe in slowly and exhale. I send a sarcastic reply to the group along the lines of "being famous" while I pull myself together. Once I'm sure I'm not going to be sick, I get back on the road. I have an appointment with my therapist to get to, and I feel like I for sure need it now.

I've still been posting a song each day on Facebook and my song for today is "It's Not Over Yet" by for King and Country.

The lyrics talk about the voices in your head that tell you you're not going to win this time and you won't find freedom—how there's a war that rages, and you constantly feel beaten down and already defeated. The song is written for those who think they've hit their limit and reminds them that the race isn't finished yet. It gives encouragement to keep fighting and to not give up. It's very fitting for my situation, but most of me just wants all this over.

> *"Therefore, since we also have such a large cloud of witnesses surrounding us, let us lay aside every weight and the sin that so easily ensnares us. Let us run with endurance the race that lies before us, keeping our eyes on Jesus, the source and perfecter of our faith, who for the joy that lay before Him endured a cross and despised the shame and has sat down at the right hand of God's throne."*
> *Hebrews 12:1-2 HCSB*

Friday, July 8th, 2022

THE SONG I POST TODAY is "Eye of the Storm" by Ryan Stevenson. Speaking of eyes, my left eye continues to get red and irritated off and on. I'm not sure what's going on with it. I don't have time to worry about it. My "bonus daughter" is having surgery today, and I've got plenty to take care of for work in addition to getting one of my boys to a hair appointment.

As I'm working on dinner, my other son comes home from work, and I ask him how his day was. "Not great," he mumbles. "I got fired."

"Oh no!" I exclaim. "What happened?"

"They said I wasn't a fit," he responds.

I know he didn't care for the job, but it was only for the summer. He wasn't going to be able to keep it once he started his college classes. He needs to stay busy, though, and he's not very motivated to actually find a job. Now I know his dad and I will have to busy ourselves with trying to help him find work again. *Sigh…*

> *"Trust in the LORD with all your heart, and do not rely on your own understanding; think about Him in all your ways, and He will guide you on the right paths." Proverbs 3:5-6 HCSB*

Sunday, July 10th, 2022

TOMORROW THE YOUNGEST OF MY kids becomes an "adult," and the song I post is "Better Than a Hallelujah" by Amy Grant. This is a great song that reminds us that it's not always "Hallelujahs" we're crying, but sometimes there are only tears, and grief, and that's okay. God just wants to hear from us. It's okay to pour our breaking hearts out to Him.

With this boy, there have been more tears and miseries than hallelujahs, and I must trust that God has kept up with those tears.

I've also been posting a verse each day. Today I post Joshua 1:9, which reads, "Haven't I commanded you: be strong and courageous? Do not be afraid or discouraged, for the LORD your God is with you wherever you go" (HCSB).

This is one of my favorite verses and it's the one I claimed for this son when he first moved in with us. In fact, I had the Hebrew word for "Strong," which is used in this verse, tattooed on me. I told him I prayed that he would always be strong, not just in physical strength, but in character and trust in the Lord, as well. He says he wants the same tattoo but can't seem to save enough money to go get it. He's also been in a lot of scary places already in his short life, and I know he'll probably be in more. I want him to know that *wherever* he is, God is there with him, even when he can't feel Him. He still has *much* growing to do, but this is still my prayer for him, and I think he knows that wherever he goes, not only will the Lord be with him, but a piece of my heart will be as well.

We've also decided to give him the keys to his truck back for his birthday. I'm crossing my fingers that it lasts for a while.

> *"Haven't I commanded you: be strong and courageous? Do not be afraid or discouraged, for the L*ORD *your God is with you wherever you go." Joshua 1:9 HCSB*

Monday, July 18ᵗʰ, 2022

I'M AT A DOCTOR'S APPOINTMENT with the lady I help when a text comes through my phone from my son. "I just got fired." This would be the son that still had a job, at least until now anyway. We still haven't found a new job for the other son. I guess I'm now job-searching for both of them. *Good grief!* I don't know how I'm ever going to get these two to become independent.

The song I post today is Jason Gray's "Remind Me Who I Am." I hope these boys remember who they are. I even must be reminded of who I am at times. This song speaks to me when I find myself in lonely places, when I don't like what I see in the mirror, when I forget what grace is. This song tells us to go to God and have Him tell us who we are, as He only speaks the truth. Sometimes, our hearts get callous, and I've had kids run far from God; I need Him to remind them who they are. We all need help believing that we really are God's beloved and that we really are "enough." I pray all my kids will receive this truth and His love.

> *"For you formed my inward parts; you knitted me together in my mother's womb. I praise you, for I am fearfully and wonderfully made. Wonderful are your works; my soul knows it very well. My frame was not hidden from you, when I*

was being made in secret, intricately woven in the depths of the earth. Your eyes saw my unformed substance; in your book were written, every one of them, the days that were formed for me, when as yet there was none of them." Psalm 139:13-16 ESV

Thursday, July 21st, 2022

TODAY STARTS OUT WITH ME having to drive one son to the community college for his GED training, due to his truck sitting at the mechanic's shop. The other son has an interview near the college, so I tell him he can ride with us and I'll take him to the interview. I wait in the car for him. Fortunately, I've brought my book to read. The interview is taking longer than I would expect, which I see as a good sign. Sure enough, when he comes out, he has paperwork with him, and he stammers that he got the job. "That's great!" I exclaim.

"But Mom, I don't want the job! I don't think I'll be good at this job! Please don't make me do it! I promise I'll find something else!"

I don't know whether to be frustrated, angry, or sad. I begin backing the car up. "Look," I declare, "you're going to take this job and give it a try. I think you'll be just fine at it. Plus, the hours are perfect for you to be able to keep working once your classes start."

He continues to whine and beg but I refuse to accept it. We get home; I help fill out the paperwork, give him his social security card, and tell him he must head back down there, turn in the paperwork, and accept the position. *One kid working, one more to go.*

The days have been so full and busy. The anxiety has been better, and apparently, the anti-nausea meds are working because I've picked up several pounds. I don't like seeing the numbers go up on the scale, but I remind myself I needed to gain a few. I'm always running and doing for someone, but I've started carving out more time for myself. I almost always have my reading time in the evenings, but I've managed to get away to the pool about once a week. Today, I've blocked off a couple of hours for a massage. This is a therapist who was recommended to me a year or so ago, and I've gone to see her a few times. She's good, honing right in on where you need stiffness and knots worked out.

Before she gets started, I ask if I can play my own music while she works. "Of course!" she replies. I hit "shuffle" on my playlist and the first to play is what I had posted for today: "He Knows" by Jeremy Camp. The silent tears fall while she works out the knots in my back and hums along to the music.

This song talks about being in those valleys when you don't even have the words to pray. When you're hurting in ways that no one knows about, God knows. He sees how you fight and the weight you carry. We just have to let that weight bring us to our knees and turn our eyes up to Him. This song reminds us that we're all going to go through those times of darkness and that even He went through the darkness. But He counts our tears and is near to those who are brokenhearted.

> *"And the peace of God, which surpasses every thought, will guard your hearts and minds in Christ Jesus." Philippians 4:7 HCSB*

Friday, July 22nd, 2022

MY EYE IS STILL GIVING me problems, so I do what I should have done in the first place and message my eye doctor. I take a picture of my eye and send it to her. I want to avoid having to schedule an appointment, if possible; my days are just too full. I tell her how long it's been going on and the drops I've already tried. She responds with, "It's episcleritis. It's inflammatory and is related to excessive stress. I'll call you in some drops, but you probably want to stay out of your contacts if possible."

Stress?! I don't have any stress!

> *"Even though I walk through the valley of the shadow of death, I fear no evil, for You are with me; Your rod and Your staff, they comfort me." Psalm 23:4 NSAB*

Sunday, July 24th, 2022

I JUST SPENT TWENTY-FOUR HOURS with two of my very best friends. The song I post for today is "Carry Me" by Josh Wilson. Obviously, this song is talking about allowing God to carry you through the storms of life, but He usually accomplishes this by sending people your way to carry you. I may have a lot of storms I've gone through and am currently going through, but He has blessed me with friends.

There are times when all of us feel as if our legs will no longer carry us and we need Him to step in and do the walking for us. He gives us solid ground instead of unsteady sand. He calms our hearts and reminds us to breathe. The song is a reminder that He will never forsake us. Even when we feel certain He has left us, it's then that we will find Him carrying us.

"Just as lotions and fragrance give sensual delight, a sweet friendship refreshes the soul." Proverbs 27:9 The Message

Thursday, July 28th, 2022

IT'S A *GOOD* DAY. MY other son has started a new job. It's full-time and the right hours for him to continue to take his classes. Both boys are working again! The scripture I post for the day is an encouraging one. It comes from Romans chapter eight, and it's one I've spent a lot of time in.

I finish the day with a date with my husband, and we go to his mom's house to bring her a birthday gift. Her birthday is tomorrow, but our day is too full tomorrow. My husband has written his first book and has dedicated it to his mom. He has waited to announce it until giving it to her today for her birthday. Of course, she is delighted and proud. The title of the book is *Overcoming Anxiety: How to Live a Worry-Free Life*. We spend some time floating in the pool and talking about the book. I have a thing or two to mention about anxiety. "You should write a book someday." He tells me this all the time.

"Nah," I respond, "not really interested."

> *"What, then, shall we say in response to these things? If God is for us, who can be against us? He who did not spare his own Son, but gave him up for us all—how will He not also, along with him, graciously give us all things? Who will bring any charge against those whom God has chosen? It is God who justifies. Who then is the one who condemns? No one. Christ Jesus who died—more than that, who was raised to life—is at the right hand of God and is also interceding for us. Who shall separate us from the love of Christ? Shall trouble or hardship or persecution or famine or nakedness or danger or sword? As it is written: 'For your sake we face death all day long; we are considered as sheep to be slaughtered. No, in all these things we are more than conquerors through him who loved us. For I am convinced that neither death nor life, neither angels nor demons, neither the present nor the future, nor any powers, neither height nor depth, nor anything else in all creation, will be able to separate us*

from the love of God that is in Christ Jesus our Lord." Romans 8:31-39 HCSB

Tuesday, August 2nd, 2022

MY LIFE IS A WHIRLWIND right now as I try to redo everything I had done before the June 27th hearing. I'm trying to be sure everything is taken care of, just in case. I have a morning appointment to head to, but I take my son's medicine up to him to wake him up before I leave and make sure he's getting himself ready for class. I notice a few items in his room that give me red flags that he may be stealing. I voice my concerns to him, but he has his stories of how he obtained the items. I'm still suspicious, but I don't have the time or energy to deal with it right now. As I'm leaving, I state, "I'm not going to argue with you about this but if you're stealing, you'll eventually get caught, and they will press charges. You're also an adult now. Repercussions are more severe."

He gets angry and defensive. Another red flag. I can't deal with it right now, so I head out. I have a doctor's appointment for myself, and then I have to get someone else to one. I've just finished those up, and I'm answering a few work emails when I see a call coming through from my son. I check the clock; he should be at work right now. I answer it. "Hello?"

There's nothing but sobbing on the other line.

"Are you okay?" I ask while quickly checking his location. Yep, he's at work.

"You were right. Right about everything." The words come out broken and difficult to understand. He breaks down sobbing again.

My heart leaps up in my throat. I know exactly what's happened. "You didn't win those items in a contest, did you?"

"No!" He cries.

"And you just got fired?"

"Yes! I don't know what to do! I feel like I should go drive my truck off a cliff or something!"

"Stop! You need to just sit there for a minute and catch your breath. You can choose to learn from this and grow. You shouldn't let giving up be an option. Take your time getting home."

I know he will be fine once he has a chance to process things. He can say and do things impulsively, but I know him well enough to know he's going to want to come home and give me a hug. I wander into the kitchen to start dinner. I feel like I should be able to pour myself a drink or something. I have no idea what I'm going to do with this one, no idea if he's ever going to learn. It's back to the drawing board, again, on looking for a job for him. He needs to find one before this hits his record. I didn't ask him, but I'm sure they'll be pressing charges. *Good grief, I don't have time for this!*

> *"When all has been heard, the conclusion of the matter is: fear God and keep His commands, because this is for all humanity. For God will bring every act to judgment, including every hidden thing, whether good or evil." Ecclesiastes 12:13-14 HCSB*

Wednesday, August 3rd, 2022

COURT IS NOT UNTIL THIS afternoon but one of my boys has an intake appointment with a new counselor. The session is taking forever, and I start to worry that I'm not going to have time to get everything done. I like the guy, though, and

I scribble a note to tell him about my other boy. They both need all the help they can get. Once we get done, I grab lunch for us and head home. I busy myself with all the last-minute things like changing my voicemail and putting auto-replies on my email accounts. *Gosh, I hope I'm able to change those back before the day is over.*

I put my purple dress back on and make myself presentable. My husband is doing better than he was for the last hearing. I let him know I'm ready to go, and we head to the car. This time, I've put two bottles of water in my purse and something for my anxiety. I have no idea how many people may show up this time. Several who were at the last hearing have told me they can't be there today, but several others who couldn't make it last time can come this time.

We arrive at the courthouse and snake our way through the metal detectors and up to the third floor. There are already friends there to greet me. My attorney is there, and he lets me know that the defense attorney is already there as well. "I'm glad he figured out he has to be here this time," I say, not hiding the sarcasm.

When 1:30 p.m. hits, the bailiff ushers us all into the courtroom. There are more people this time and almost no space for everyone to get seats. Fortunately, things get started on time. Juror #8 is there, and after we're sworn in to testify, all preliminary discussions are taken care of and then the State enters the transcripts of the voir dire and the May 11th hearing as evidence. This time there's no objection.

The prosecutor then proceeds to read word-for-word every instruction given by the previous judge during voir dire. Also admitted as evidence is a transcript from the hearing that was held with Juror #8 when she testified to my misconduct. The entirety of that testimony is read. The prosecutor then moves on to the transcript from the May

11th hearing; the entirety of my testimony is read and she insists on reading my responses in a sarcastic, arrogant tone. *Cute,* I think, *real cute.* This entire process takes about forty-five minutes. Sitting and listening to her simply read, word-for-word, for forty-five minutes is grueling. I sip on my water and decide I need something for my anxiety.

The prosecutor then calls a circuit clerk employee to testify about how much jurors were paid for the trial. It takes a while for her to explain the calculations, but the total comes to $3,850 for all fifty or so people who showed up for jury duty.

My attorney then calls Juror #8 to testify. There's lots of arguing back and forth between the prosecutor, my attorney, and the judge regarding what can be asked, how it can be asked, and what's relevant. I can tell that my attorney is basically trying to establish that the judge was never defined as a participant in the case, nor was the victim defined as a party to the case. He doesn't get very far with any of it. Before he finishes with Juror #8, he asks her why she didn't report this while we were all there for the trial, as she was instructed. She rambles that there wasn't really an opportunity to do it discreetly, and she was afraid everyone would view her as tattling. *Nice,* I think, *this is ridiculous.*

The judge dismisses her but tells her to remain in the court room. My attorney then calls me. I swallow hard and force my legs, which seem to be encased in cement, to make their way to the stand. I have tunnel vision and can't really discern people or details in the room.

> Q: Would you please state your name and juror number for the record.
> A: Katrina Robertson, Number 11.
> Q: And in your own words, could you tell the judge what you did in this case?

A: As far as why I'm sitting here? Or just that I was a juror in the case?

Q: Well, what research did you do?

A: I researched the victim on public records, Court Connect. We had been instructed not to research the case, the parties of the case as they were read. I didn't define the victim as a party of the case due to him not being part of voir dire or being present in the courtroom. I felt as if I had…this case left me with a lot of questions. I knew I couldn't research the case, the attorneys, any of the witnesses, the defendant. I felt like looking the victim up was a loophole. I now recognize it was wrong and I wish I hadn't done it.

Q: So, you thought you found a loophole?

A: A way to…I'm a researcher by nature and I don't…I took this role as a jury member very, very seriously. It weighed heavy on me. I wanted to get my vote right. And like I said, the reason why I made the statement that…you know, and I even reached out to both the defense attorney and said I'd reach out to the judge because there were so many unanswered questions.

Q: Now was that during the trial or after the trial?

A: When I reached out? After. After the trial.

Q: Okay.

A: I never reached out…I tried to reach out to the judge but he didn't respond. Of course, I found out later why he didn't. But I just…I felt like ultimately it was irrelevant. I made that statement after we had…

Q: Don't say at what point.

A: Okay.

Q: Now, do you acknowledge now what you did was wrong, and you violated that rule?

A: Of course.

Q: And is there anything you want to tell the judge about you and rules?

A: I'm a, as was disclosed, I'm a financial planner. Specifically, I'm the chief compliance officer at my firm. It's literally my job to make sure people follow the rules. I have the utmost respect for the Courts and the laws they're tasked with upholding. I've been in courtrooms on many occasions for various reasons. In fact, in this very room as this judge granted me guardianship for my severely disabled son. But I've served in lots of capacities in courtrooms, and I have great respect for the system.

I've got five children and I have taught them to always follow rules and respect authority and I failed to do that. And the fact that I've got a courtroom here full of people—

My voice catches and I realize it's going to be painful for me to continue as I survey everyone's eyes on me. I take a deep breath and try to push on.

—who have taken their time out who love me and support me and are watching me at my literal lowest moment.

The judge, as was read in the transcript, asked me on May 11th how

what I had done made me feel and my
only response was it had tormented my
soul. That I would cause undue burden
and inconvenience to the State, to the
defendant, to the Court, to the court
reporters…and when I asked to read a
statement, it was simply an apology. I
wanted to apologize to my fellow jurors.

The tears are now falling freely, but I've been able to
find my voice.

When the question was asked, "Did you
realize what you were doing was wrong?"
I struggled with my response to that, and
I said there's a fine line. That fine line was
I thought I'd found a loophole with just
looking the victim up and nobody else. I
honestly said it so openly because I didn't
think anything of it. If I had realized that
singular statement would have put us all
where we are today, I would take it back.

It has affected me. I've had to start
counseling and start taking meds. It's
obviously cost me financially. Mental and
emotional health. And so many people…
this is the second time so many people
have sat in this courtroom for me, and
I've just been humbled by the entire
experience.

My attorney says he'll pass the witness.
The prosecutor stands.

Q: Ms. Robertson, I respect your apology. Thank
you. But in my job, I'm supposed to do what's
fair and right, and I want you to look to the
right. Would you agree with me that that's a
woman who didn't get a fair jury by her peers?

I don't give a verbal answer to this. There's no way I can
answer honestly without getting myself in more trouble. The
truth is I believe her peers gave her a very fair trial, but I don't
believe the system did. This hearing is about me, though, and
not the system.

Q: Did you follow the rules?
A: I'm having trouble answering that because that
statement played no role in the deliberations.
Q: Did you follow the rules?
A: In my mind, I did. At that time. I now recognize
that I did not.
Q: So, when the judge says, "Do not do your own
research," twice before you deliberated, you
heard that, but you just didn't consider it?
A: I didn't think looking the victim up would be
that big of a deal.
Q: Now Ms. Robertson, we spent a whole week
together and I showed you a lot of pictures of
her husband in a wheelchair, you saw pictures
of the crime scene, and you're telling me today
that you didn't think he was a party to this?
A: I didn't think it would be relevant if I looked it
up.
Q: Don't you think that if I had something to show
I would've given it to you?
A: Absolutely.

My mind is reeling. I want to shout, "No, you wouldn't have given us criminal records on the victim; you're the prosecutor!" I believe the defense attorney wanted to give testimony of the victim's character and abusive nature, but we have no way of knowing if that was the testimony that wasn't allowed.

> Q: Would you agree with me that there are Rules of Criminal Procedure and Rules of Evidence and that the judge can decide what you hear and what you don't hear?
>
> A: And when you're on the jury, you're tasked with the role of being the judge.
>
> Q: Please answer my question.
>
> A: You'll have to restate it.
>
> Q: Aren't there Rules of Evidence and Rules of Criminal Procedure that govern things in a courtroom?
>
> A: And I don't understand them all.
>
> Q: Okay. Okay, I understand that.
>
> A: And I don't…
>
> Q: But you did see us stand at that bench and argue a lot at that bench, wouldn't you say?
>
> A: Uh-hum.
>
> Q: Don't you think that we were arguing about those rules—those Rules of Evidence and whether things should be presented to the jury or not?
>
> A: And I felt that as a jury, we should have access to all information.
>
> Q: So even though the judge decided you didn't have a right to hear it under the Rules of

Criminal Procedure and Rules of Evidence, you
knew better than him, right?

A: No. I just thought if I'm tasked with the...
having to determine another individual's guilt
or innocence that I should be able to have access
to all the information.

Q: So, you didn't hear the part where he said you
will not second guess my decisions? That you
will make your decision on the evidence that is
before you and the facts that are before you? You
didn't hear that part in his instruction either?

A: That's exactly what I made my decision on. Only
on the facts that were presented in the case,
period. I stand by the vote and all deliberation
a hundred percent. It was only on the evidence
that was presented.

Q: But you realize that what you did has set all that
aside? You do realize that today, right?

A: Of course.

That's my answer, but what I want to say is that a juror
complaining and a judge deciding on a mistrial set all that
aside. My actions should not have caused this.

Q: She has to be tried again because you didn't
follow the rules. You testified earlier that you
tried to reach out to the judge during the trial?

A: No, absolutely I did not say that. Afterwards.

Q: Afterwards, you tried to reach out and he did
not...

A: Respond.

Q: Contact you then?

A: Correct.

The prosecutor finally says that she has no further questions.

At this point, the judge takes over the questioning. My mouth is dry, and I wish I had my water.

> The Court: Okay, Ms. Robertson, I'm having a hard time understanding you. You said that you didn't think you broke any of the rules because something about a participant. That you didn't consider the deceased victim in this case to be a party to the case and that you over-analyze things and that you didn't think you broke the rules. But then you said to the jurors, "I can't be the only one who broke the rules."
>
> A: I don't recall that.
>
> The Court: Which is it? Well, that's what they said.
>
> A: Well, that's what they said.
>
> The Court: Well, which is it?
>
> A: Like I said when you asked me that question and I said that there's a fine line, because, at that point, I didn't see it as breaking the rules. But then sitting where I'm sitting now on May 11th, I absolutely knew it was.
>
> The Court: So, you're telling me that you went into the whole trial considering whatever the judge said to be just, "Maybe I should follow that? If I don't think I should follow it, then I don't have to follow it?" Is that the way you went into the trial?
>
> A: Of course not.
>
> The Court: Well, isn't that what you just said? That you over-analyze things. That you thought that information was important, and it hadn't been

given to you, you thought, as the decider of the facts that you should have all the information, whether it came from this room or whether you went out and found it on your own? You just said that.

I'm having trouble controlling my facial expressions at this point as she continually puts words in my mouth. I realize I'm going to have to be very careful in my answers with her as it will be easy for me to become sarcastic and disrespectful.

In other words, even though the judge told you, "You're not allowed to consider anything but the evidence produced in this trial?"

A: And I didn't consider anything else.

The Court: You did. You did independent research. Went outside this courtroom, that courtroom, and you decided on your own that you needed the answer to another question that hadn't been presented in the evidence. You looked it—

A: But it didn't play…

The Court: Don't interrupt me. You looked it up. Decided for yourself. "This is something I need to share with my fellow jurors" and then indeed shared it with your fellow jurors. That's correct, isn't it? By the way, do you have gum in your mouth? Would you please take it out. So isn't that correct, that you decided, "I want to know this, the judge has told me I'm not allowed to find out but I'm gonna do it anyway because I need to know as the trier of fact?"

A: I guess I'm a bad jury member.

The Court: I didn't ask you that question. I said isn't that what you just said you did?

I can tell she's just going to continue to twist my words and badger me, so I don't really respond.

The Court: And if you can't answer that question, then let me ask you this: Why did you think that you should substitute your knowledge for the orders of the Court, the attorneys who were trying the case, and impart that to the jury? How in the world could you think that was a proper thing to do?

A: I feel like everything I have to say at this particular point is going to be used against me.

The Court: Well, I mean you don't have to say anything. You started out by saying that you were sorry, but I'm not sure I understand what you think you did that you thought was wrong.

A: I've said, I recognize now that it was wrong, and I'm apologizing.

The Court: But do you see the difference there when you say "I recognize it now because now I've been held…I've been given a 'show cause' order, but, at the time, I didn't do anything wrong?" You see what I mean? You're saying on the one hand, "Yeah, I know that we're all here because of me," but on the other hand—

A: It…

The Court: Don't interrupt me, ma'am. I'm talking. Do you recognize my position here? Do I get that recognition that I am the judge here?

A: Yes.

The Court: Okay. Then can I finish my statement before you say something? The point is if you're conciliatory and understand the mistake that you made and are sorry for it and believe that you did something wrong, that's one thing. But to say that "At the time I didn't think...I didn't do anything wrong, I wanted to know this information, I looked it up on the internet, I shared it with my fellow jurors in contradiction to every instruction that I was given by the Court and now I see that that's what caused all this." Do you see how they're different? You're not really taking the blame, are you?

A: There are nine other jury members that aren't here to testify to not even recalling me saying anything.

The Court: Are you denying you said it?

A: I am not, I'm just saying it was insignificant at the moment. I didn't think it—

Apparently, she's allowed to interrupt me.

The Court: That's not the point. Do we look at the result of our conduct to determine whether it was rightfully done? Because the argument you're giving me is if I shoot at somebody, but I miss them, then it's okay. Do you see?

Actually, I don't see and all I can do is stare at her and blink. I have no idea the analogy she's trying to convey.

That's the argument you're giving me. "In the big scheme of things, I didn't

> really do anything wrong because there
> were nine other jurors, and they might
> not have heard me." Do you see what I
> mean?
>
> You did the act. You've admitted
> you did the act. You've admitted that
> the judge told you multiple times in the
> court's standardized jury instructions
> that you're not allowed to do that. But
> you did it anyway.

Did I admit this? I'm so confused at her rattling on and on that I just stare.

> That's the problem. It's not whatever the
> outcome might be, even though there's a
> mistrial because of it. Do you recognize
> that? Or do you just not want to take
> responsibility for what you did?

A: Did I not take responsibility?

The Court: I'm just not sure, that's what I'm saying.
You say that you only think now that you did
something wrong. And when you said to the
other jurors, "I can't believe I'm the only one
who broke the rules…"

A: I don't recall that.

The Court: Everyone said you said that.

A: Nine other jurors did not.

The Court: Okay. Okay, we'll go back again to the
very thing that we started with. Do you not
think you did anything wrong?

A: I do now.

I'm exhausted now and don't think she will ever finish badgering me.

> The Court: But you didn't then? You want me to believe that you didn't think you did anything wrong at the time that you said, "I can't be the only one who broke the rules?" And even if you want to say you didn't say that, you knew you went out on the internet to a public internet site and looked up the criminal histories of the people involved in the case, a murder case. And then you relayed it. You didn't keep it to yourself. You relayed that information to your fellow jurors.
>
> A: And I—

She cuts me off, but I want to say that I believe my fellow jurors know what information could be used in deliberations and what couldn't be.

> The Court: Who, by the way, was so upset about it that the next morning had to go into the judge's office and put themselves in front of the judge and say something happened.

"But yet didn't have the nerve to say it during deliberations," I wanted to interject.

> Do you still believe that you only now know that something was wrong? Because I kinda need to know whether you're accepting responsibility at the time that you did it or only now because of what happened.

A: I mean, yeah, I accept the responsibility that I did it and I absolutely shouldn't have, and I regret it immensely.

The Court: And you knew it?

Good grief, she's not going to give up.

A: I mean I guess, on some level, because I said I was searching for a loophole, you know.

The Court: "On some level," so I'm supposed to search what level you accept responsibility at the time that you did this? You see, it's a contempt charge and so contempt is all about disobeying Court's orders. Because this room has a certain integrity to it and unless the integrity of this room is maintained, then there's no law and order, isn't that right? I mean do you agree with me on that?

A: Yes.

The Court: Unless we say, as a group, that this room is about truth, that we're striving to get to the truth and that we have to have integrity in this room, we have to tell the truth, we have to assume that people are telling us the truth; otherwise, we have a flawed system. Do you agree with that?

A: Yes.

The Court: So, when you tell me, "Only now afterwards because I see what happened, do I think that I did anything wrong," that's not really true, is it?

A: I don't...I guess at the time I thought I should be privileged to more information and I...you know, I mean I guess that was wrong.

The Court: Because it was in violation of the Court's orders to you on many, many occasions during the trial.

A: Yeah.

Just keep answering yes and maybe this will end, I think.

The Court: Isn't that right?

A: Yeah.

The Court: So, in spite of what the Court told you, you thought you should have that information, and by God, you were going to get it. Is that what you're telling me?

A: And I guess there were still so many things that I felt like I didn't have information to, and I made sure that I didn't research those things. I guess that's where I'm going. I felt like—

The Court: So you knew, you knew that you weren't allowed.

A: I felt like—

The Court: You knew you weren't allowed to do that, and you did it anyway. But you didn't think this one was as important as the other ones?

A: Sure.

She's not going to accept any answer other than what she wants and is going to continually cut me off.

The Court: Is that what you're telling me?

A: Yeah.

The Court: But do you recognize that no matter what you thought was important didn't matter? That the Court is the decider of what's important, the attorneys are the decider of what's important, this room is the decider of what's important, not you. Do you admit that? I mean do you acknowledge that?

A: Sure.

The Court: And when you took an oath to try that case fairly and to follow the Court's instruction, you violated that oath. Is that right?

A: Yeah.

Finally, the judge asks if any of the attorneys have questions for me, and they don't, so she says I may step down. Then she resumes speaking.

The Court: Well, I mean obviously the admission by Ms. Robertson that she has committed contempt is the finding of the Court that in fact contempt was committed. That she knowingly, willfully committed the contempt.

Pretty sure that wasn't my testimony.

That this contempt is punishable by up to thirty days in the county jail

Wait, my attorney said up to a year? I guess it doesn't matter at this point.

and/or a fine of up to five hundred dollars. It's a Class C misdemeanor.

This Court finds you guilty of that misdemeanor. You're fined five hundred dollars. There's a tremendous amount of restitution that goes into a four-day trial. There are expert witnesses who are paid by both sides to come into the courtroom and they're paid by the hour and when there's a mistrial because of juror misconduct, those have to be done again. There are attorney's fees that add up. The defendant had a private attorney and a tremendous amount of attorney's fees that will have to be paid again because of the mistrial that you caused.

There's court time which takes the place of other people trying to get into the courtroom, trying to have their cases heard, and now another five-day trial will have to be held because of your misconduct.

There are many, many, many, many reasons why the rules are what the rules are. And it's not for us, in any particular role, to decide for ourselves why we don't have to obey those rules. Because if everybody in the system doesn't do what the rules require them to do, then the end result is a lack of justice. And if there's one thing about this room, it's about the seeking of justice.

I want to laugh at this. This room is obviously about rules that often prevent justice.

That's what we've been trying to do. That's what we do every day in this room. It's not about the individual and what you feel or want, or think is about you. It's about seeking justice. And we do it according to a certain set of rules and laws and we all agree and take an oath to abide by those laws. I took an oath, the prosecutor takes an oath, and attorneys take an oath. If anybody doesn't abide by their rules and their laws and their oath, then justice is not the end result. And that's what happened here.

So now we must try this case again which means we have to get another jury and we will have to pay, the taxpayers of this county will have to pay for another jury all because of what you chose to do on that day. So, you will pay restitution in the amount of $3,850. That's the amount of money that the taxpayers in our county paid for the jurors in this case.

All right, all of this is due this day. Do you intend to pay it today?

I respond that I will, and the hearing is concluded.

Everyone stands and forms a line to give me a hug as they leave. The tears are falling again. They're all telling me they're glad it's over for me. My attorney tells me to meet him back at his office, and he'll get the order for me.

My husband and I get to the attorney's office, and he hands me the order with the fine and restitution I have to pay and tells me where to go to pay it. That brings the total to nearly $8,000 that I've had to spend on this. I don't bother asking him about the thirty days versus the one-year jail time. I'm just too exhausted. I thank him for his time and help. My husband and I head back to the courthouse to pay the restitution. When we get to the courthouse, they have no idea how to handle the restitution payment. It's obvious they've never seen an order like this. They tell me I can go on over to the sheriff's office to pay my fine and then come back over and maybe they will have it figured out.

We wander over to the sheriff's office and take care of that and then head back to the courthouse. They're right next to each other, but I'm not exactly dressed for all this hiking through parking lots and buildings. I'm ready to take my heels off.

We get back to the courthouse and they take a check from me and produce a copy of both the check and the order and give me a receipt. I'm not sure they know what to do with it from there, but I've done my part.

At this point, it's nearly dinner time and I'm hungry. Since we're both dressed up and I'm certainly not cooking tonight, I tell my husband we should go to a nice restaurant and celebrate. He agrees.

He drops me off in front of a high-end restaurant in our downtown area while he goes to find a parking spot. I take a seat and the waiter approaches.

"Celebrating a special occasion this evening?" he asks.

I pause. *Should I just be honest with him? Aren't I always honest with people? Why stop now?* "Well, I just got out of court and didn't get jail time so yes, we're celebrating."

The waiter laughs and holds his hand up for a high five. "Now that's something to celebrate! Congratulations! I actually have court on Monday, and I'm looking at possibly thirty days, so I know exactly where you're at!" he exclaims.

I laugh and my husband joins me at the table. We look over the overpriced menu and decide on our selections. When our dinner arrives, we savor every bite.

When we arrive home, I get into comfy clothes, change my voicemail and the auto-response to my email, and retire to my chair. I have a *lot* of messages to respond to and a book I want to finish reading.

> *"He'll validate your life in the clear light of day and stamp you with approval at high noon. Quiet down before GOD, be prayerful before him. Don't bother with those who climb the ladder, who elbow their way to the top. Bridle your anger, trash your wrath, cool your pipes—it only makes things worse. Before long the crooks will be bankrupt; GOD-investors will soon own the store."*
> *Psalm 37:6-9 The Message*

Thursday, August 4th, 2022

I WAKE IN THE MORNING and wait for word on if the story is in the paper. Sure enough, my mother-in-law sends the link, "Former Juror Found in Contempt, Fined." Front page again. *Good grief.* I'm sure they will mention me again whenever the retrial finally happens, which apparently won't be until January 2023 now. *Ridiculous.* Everyone is telling me they're so glad it's over for me, but I don't feel like it will be completely over until the retrial is over. Hopefully, my life will get back to some sort of "normal" in the meantime.

> *"Now the Lord is the Spirit, and where the Spirit of the Lord is, there is freedom." 2 Corinthians 3:17 HCSB*

Monday, August 8th, 2022

MY SON IS OUT TURNING in applications for jobs when he calls and stammers that he's had a wreck. *Awesome, he didn't even last a month!* I'm glad he's okay, but I hope the car is still drivable. We can't afford a new car at this point, nor does it make sense to get him one. My husband gets word and heads that way to assist with the situation.

When they get home, my son storms off walking, in the rain. My husband comes in and says he'd had a stern talk with him, and our son had gotten angry. My son stays gone for an hour or so, and I track him on an app to see where he's at. It rains almost the entire time.

By the time he gets back, I've already taken my place in my chair with my book. He's soaking wet, and I tell him to leave his clothes in the laundry room. Other than that, we don't speak. There's not any need to.

> *"Go ahead and be angry. You do well to be angry—but don't use your anger as fuel for revenge. And don't stay angry. Don't go to bed angry. Don't give the Devil that kind of foothold in your life." Ephesians 4:26-27 The Message*

Monday, August 15th, 2022

MY SON HAS FOUND A job and he starts tonight. It's only part-time, but it will have to do for now. I had been checking with the police department to see if his warrant had gone active for the theft, but, as of Friday, it still wasn't active. His ticket from the wreck has shown up, though, so I get him out of bed to take him down to the courthouse to take care of that. I tell him it makes sense to just go pay the fine rather than go to court. He gets dressed, and we head down there.

We get to the clerk's window, he gives her his information so she can look it up, and then she asks a few more questions. About then, an officer shows up behind her and glances at her computer screen. He looks up and studies my son. Suddenly, I realize what's happened. His warrant has gone active over the weekend, and an officer has been alerted. "Do you realize you have an active warrant?" the officer asks my son.

"Ummmmm…" And he turns toward me.

"I checked to see if it was active on Friday, and it wasn't. I was going to take him down to the police department to turn himself in once it was active," I reply.

"Well," he sighs, "you should have gone there first because now I don't have any choice but to take him with me."

I look at my son. "Do you understand what's going to happen?" I ask.

"Not really," he says nervously.

"He has to take you into custody and probably take you to the detention center."

I get his traffic ticket paid and we shuffle into the hall with the officer. The officer tells me I can get my son's phone from the car. When I get back inside with his phone, the officer has already taken my son to the holding cell. The officer takes the phone and tells me that, if I can wait a little bit, he'll let me know if my son is going to the detention center or the police department. I had grabbed my phone as well, so I take a seat and scroll Facebook while I wait. My feed is almost nothing but friends getting their kids settled in at college with their dorms all looking perfect. My eyes begin to burn, and a lump rises in my throat. Most of the captions with the photos include crying emojis and moms declaring how sad it is that their baby has grown up and moved to college. I turn the phone off and set it on my lap and allow the tears to fall. *Do these parents have any idea how blessed they are to be able to settle their kids into a college dorm? I'm getting ready to have to bond mine out of jail.* Five kids, and although one has gotten her associate's degree, none will ever go "away" to college. Sometimes, you just must let a dream go.

The officer comes back out and lets me know that they're transferring him to the detention center and I can head down there and bond him out if I want. I thank him and let him know I will as soon as I go to another appointment. He radios to the center and tells them I'll be down in a couple of hours and to not bother dressing him out.

The appointment I have is with my therapist. As I sit down with her and begin to tell her about my morning, my phone rings and I see it's from the detention center. I tell her it's my son and I need to answer it. He's crying and asks when I'm coming. I tell him in an hour or two. I finish up my appointment and tell my therapist that I think I'm going to write a book about my experiences. "I would like to read it," she comments as I leave.

I head to the detention center and let them know why I'm there and they direct me to a door I can go through to get the bond paid and sign some papers. I head back there and can't believe I'm here, again. I've now come to the detention center to either visit or bond out all three of my adopted sons. This was certainly not how I had imagined things would go with them. After I've paid the bond, signed the papers, and waited a bit, my phone rings and I see it's my son. "Hey, I'm out front," he says. I head that way and meet my son outside.

"Thank you," he stutters as we head to the car.

"You know the only reason I bonded you out is because you start that new job tonight and you've been working diligently in your GED class?"

"I know," he replies somberly.

"If there's a next time, you'll have to stay in there until your court date."

"I understand."

"Do you remember how bad it tore me up to have to leave your brother in jail?" I ask while I hold back tears.

"I do."

"Please don't put me through that again."

"I won't. I promise," he whispers while giving my leg a rub.

> *"The Spirit of the Lord G*OD *is on Me, because the L*ORD *has anointed Me to bring good news to the poor. He has sent Me to heal the brokenhearted, to proclaim liberty to the captives and freedom to the prisoners."*
> *Isaiah 61:1 HSCB*

Saturday, September 10th, 2022

LIFE HAS CONTINUED TO BRING various trials each day, some big, some small. For the most part, I take them with ease. I have a fairly lazy Saturday planned and my husband and I are going to a concert tonight. As I'm going through my chores, I begin to get notifications from friends and family that I'm in the paper again. I sit down at my computer so I can pull the article up. I hold my breath. The title reads, "Wife Sentenced to 10 Years in Husband's Death." *Wait,* I think, *did the new trial happen?!* I read through the article; they talk bad about me. I realize that the State decided to offer her a plea deal for manslaughter, and she took it. There will be no new trial. Just like that, it seems the nightmare has ended.

I sit back and let that soak in. A lesser charge is what I wanted for her all along, and now she has it. I wonder why the State decided to offer such a lesser plea to her. They talk about how complicated a new trial would be given my misconduct. *Do they just not want to mess with it, or did my "misconduct" expose all the holes in their case? Was the defense attorney somehow able to use the mistrial to argue for a plea deal for manslaughter?* Maybe someday, I'll have answers to some of my questions. For now, I'm just glad that it's behind me.

My husband and I head to an upscale restaurant that's close to the venue for the concert, which is about an hour from our home. The dinner is great, and our table is even better. We're seated outside with a great view and a cool breeze while we enjoy our meal. My mind keeps wandering to all that has transpired over the past several months and trying to grasp that it's over. My husband asks several times if I'm okay. I then realize what I need to do. I need to write.

"So be content with who you are, and don't put on airs. God's strong hand is on you; he'll promote you at the right time. Live carefree before God; he is most careful with you." 1 Peter 5:6-7 The Message

Sunday, September 11ᵗʰ, 2022

MY HUSBAND AND I HAD stayed out-of-town last night. We take our time getting up this morning (I got a late checkout), and I spent some time reading at the pool before we pack up and head home. When we get home, I feel fully focused to sit down and write out all the events from the past several months. I pull my calendar up and begin remembering each day, most filled with notes and appointments for the day, and I use it to jog my memory. As I begin to write, the memories and emotions keep coming at rapid speed, in torrents from deep in my soul, heart, and mind. I pour it all out, attempting to purge myself of all the pain. It also doesn't escape me that today is the anniversary of 9/11, another day with memories etched in my mind. That's a day we should never forget, and we should always learn from it. I feel like my recent life experiences should also not be forgotten and that I should learn from them. Maybe others can learn from them, too?

In the meantime, I'm retired from jury duty, forever.

"So do not fear, for I am with you; do not be dismayed, for I am your God. I will strengthen you and help you; I will uphold you with my righteous right hand." Isaiah 41:10 NIV

Epilogue

A TWIST IN THE STORY and an update is that I reached out to the defendant via electronic message to the jail she was being held at once I knew the case was closed. I wanted her to know I was writing a book about the whole experience. Her response to me began with: "YHWH (Hebrew ... Self-Existent One) has used you to preserve my life. No matter what happens, I'll be thanking Him for you forever."

Since that time, we've communicated and visited on a regular basis. As always, I tend to find friends in unlikely individuals in unlikely places. What I've learned is sung about in the song, "Fix My Eyes" by for King and Country. It talks about loving people, even when you're scared and when things aren't fair, give anyway. Live your life for others, and when you see a brother or sister in need, take time for them. When freedom is needed, speak out. When someone is unable to fight for themselves, fight for them. You'll have battles but find your faith during them. Just remember to continue to RISE! Regarding the defendant, she has her own story to tell and her own battle she is learning to RISE from.

Afterword

As I've waded through various trying times, I've had well-meaning people tell me, "God will never give you more than you can handle." I call nonsense on that. God has continuously, my entire life, given me more than I can handle. If I could handle it on my own, what purpose would He serve? Instead, He gives me just enough grace for each day. I've learned about true faith, unseeing faith, faith that holds to promises when nothing else makes sense, faith that says I will follow Him "even if…" I've learned that even when life isn't good, God is still great. I've learned that you can pour your soul into a dream and see it swept away, but you should still chase the dream. And above all, I've learned that a person's character and integrity are by far their most precious assets. And to quote 1 Corinthians 13:13 (HCSB), "Now these three remain: faith, hope, and love. But the greatest of these is love."

Still, this whole ordeal left me sad that our system of "justice" is not what I thought it was. I always knew the system could be manipulated, but now I know just how much it can be manipulated. The rules in the system are there to protect people, but people learn how to use the rules to manipulate and to do the opposite of their intent. Thus, we see a division between the spirit of the law and the letter of the law.

My reason for writing this is simply to tell my story from my perspective. Others who were involved in this story no doubt have different perspectives. It's not my intent to vilify any of the people in this story; my nature is to believe that they were all doing what they believed to be in the best interest of whomever they were serving: their client, the State, their job, and even themselves. I went back and forth on putting my story out there, forever worried that the facts disclosed may offend someone. Maybe my story will bring new insight into some of the weaknesses of the system and how these areas can be addressed.

More importantly, my hope is that my story will encourage others to push through their own "trials" in their lives, continue to RISE, and share their own stories of how they've overcome.

> *"Therefore we do not give up. Even though our outer person is being destroyed, our inner person is being renewed day by day. For our momentary light affliction is producing for us an absolutely incomparable eternal weight of glory. So we do not focus on what is seen, but on what is unseen. For what is seen is temporary, but what is unseen is eternal." 2 Corinthians 4:16-18 HCSB*

> *"The fundamental fact of existence is that this trust in God, this faith, is the firm foundation under everything that makes life worth living. It's our handle on what we can't see. The act of faith is what distinguished our ancestors, set them above the crowd." Hebrews 11:1-2 The Message*

"Just like moons and like suns, with the certainty of tides, just like hopes springing high, Still I'll rise." ~ *Maya Angelou*

Made in the USA
Columbia, SC
28 May 2023

17073154R00117